Published by Peripeteia Press Ltd.

First published March 2019

ISBN: 978-1-9997376-7-2

Check out our A-level English Literature website, peripeteia.webs.com

The Art of Drama, vol. 1

An Inspector Calls

Contents

Introduction to *The Art of Drama* series

The philosopher Nietzsche described his work as 'the greatest gift that [mankind] has ever been given'. The Elizabethan poet Edmund Spenser hoped his book *The Faerie Queene* would magically transform its readers into noblemen. In comparison, our aims for *The Art of Drama* series of books are a little more modest. Fundamentally we aim to provide books that will be of maximum use to English students and to their teachers. In our experience, few students read essays on literary texts, yet, whatever specification they are studying, English students have to write analytical essays. So, we're offering some models, written in a lively and accessible style.

In this new series of books, we aim to reproduce the success of our *The Art of Poetry* series by providing fine-grained, well-informed and engaging material on the key issues in key GCSE set texts. In the first book in the series, we focus on J. B. Priestley's popular old stager, *An Inspector Calls*. Future books in the series will include critical guides to *Macbeth* and other plays that feature frequently on examination syllabi.

As with our poetry books, we hope this new series will appeal to all teachers and students of Literature. However, there is a plethora of material already available on *An Inspector Calls* on the market. Our critical guide is distinguished by our focus on complete essays and on our aim to stimulate students aiming for level 7 and above in their English Literature GCSE.

This book is arranged into four parts: introductory material, critical appreciation of key scenes, exemplar essays and teaching & revision ideas.

Writing about plays

The play and the novel

Plays and novels have several features in common, such as characters, dialogue, plots and settings. In addition, pupils read plays in lessons, often sitting at desks in the same way as they read novels, so it's not surprising that many treat these two related, but distinct, literary art forms as if they were the same. Time and again, teachers and examiners come across sentences such as 'In the novel An Inspector Calls...' Though sometimes it can be just a slip of the pen, often this error is a sign of a weak response. Stronger responses fully appreciate the fact that An Inspector Calls is a play, written for the stage, by a playwright and appreciate the implications of the writer's choice of this form.

Characterisation

Imagine you're a novelist writing a scene introducing a major character. Sit back and survey the rich variety of means at your disposal: You could begin with a quick pen portrait of their appearance, or you could have your characters say or do something significant. Alternatively, you could use your narrator to provide comments about, and background on, the character. Then again, you might take us into the character's thoughts and reveal what's really going on inside their head.

Now imagine that you're a playwright. Sit up and survey the more limited means at your disposal. Though you could describe a character's appearance , you'd have to communicate this through stage directions, which, of course, the audience would not read nor hear[1]. The same is true for background information and narratorial style comments about the character. Unless you're going to use the dramatic device known as the soliloquy, you'll struggle to find a direct way to show what your character's really thinking. As a playwright, action and dialogue, however, are your meat and drink. For a novelist being able to write dialogue is a useful skill; for a dramatist it's essential.

In other words, in general, drama focuses our attention on the outward behaviour of characters. Skilfully done, this can, of course, also reveal interior thoughts. Nevertheless, novels more easily give access to the workings of the mind. You may have noticed this when novels are adapted into films and directors have to make the decision about whether to use a voiceover to convey the narrator or characters' thoughts. Rarely does this work well.

Settings

A novelist can move quickly and painlessly from one setting to another. One chapter of a novel could be set in Victorian London, the next on a distant planet in the distant future. The only limitation is the novelist's skill in rendering these worlds. What is true for geographical settings is also true for temporal ones. A novelist can write 'One hundred years later...' or track a character from cradle to grave or play around with narrative time, using flashbacks and flashforwards.

---

[1] We'll come back later to stage directions and the differences between reading and watching a play.

Though a little more limited, a film director can also move fairly easily between geographical and temporal settings and can cross-cut between them.

Not so a playwright. Why? Because plays are written for a physical stage, so radically changing a stage set while the action of a play is running is tricky and cumbersome. How would you go about creating a stage set for Victorian London and then how could you switch to a futurist Sci-Fi setting? You could have stage technicians dismantle and construct the different stage sets while the audience waits patiently. But wouldn't that be clumsy, and rather break the spell you'd hope your play was weaving? More likely you'd use a break, perhaps between scenes or, better, during the interval for any major re-arrangement. Practically speaking, how many different stage sets could you create for a single play? Minimalistic stage designs might allow you to employ more settings, but you'd still be far more restricted than a film director or a novelist. And then there's the cost. Theatres aren't usually loaded with money and elaborate stage sets can be expensive.

Plays tend to be written chronologically with time always moving forward. Why? Because it'd be difficult to inform the audience that a scene was set in the past. The time frame of a play also tends to be limited – days, weeks, perhaps even months, but very rarely years, decades or centuries. After all, it's not easy for an actor, or series of actors, to presents characters aging over a prolonged period.

The stage and the page

Like physicists and chemists, rugby and football players or vets and doctors, novelists and playwrights have many things in common, but they also work in distinctly different fields. You wouldn't want a chemist teaching you physics, ideally, or depend on a rugby player to score a crucial FA cup goal. Nor would you want a vet to operate on you if you were ill or for your GP to treat your darling pet. And, with only a few exceptions, nor would you want to read a novel written by a playwright or witness a play written by a novelist. Precious few writers excel in both literary forms [Samuel Beckett, Chekhov and Michael Frayn come to mind, but few others] which underlines the point about the different demands of writing for the stage and for the page.

Novels take place in the theatre of the reader's mind; plays take place on an actual stage. For the latter to happen a whole load of other people other than the writer are involved – directors, actors, designers, producers, technicians and so forth. And this takes us to the heart of another difference between reading a play, reading a novel and seeing a play on a stage.

When we're reading a novel, the novelist can fill in the details of what is happening around the dialogue, such as gestures made by the characters. When we read a play, sometimes these details are apparent from stage directions. However, we cannot see what characters are doing while other characters are speaking. When we watch a play, however, actors reveal how characters are reacting to what each other are saying, and often these reactions convey crucial information about relationships, feelings and atmosphere. Without this visual dimension it is all too easily for readers to forgot that things are happening while each character is speaking. If a play on a page is like a musical score, awaiting performance, a play on the stage is like the concert itself.

Focusing on the dramatic devices used by a playwright has a double benefit: Firstly, all good analytical literary essay concentrate on the writer's craft; secondly, such a focus emphasises to the examiner that you understand the nature of the type of text you're exploring, a play, and distinguishes you from many other readers who don't really appreciate this fact. In the next section we'll sharpen our focus on the playwright's craft by honing in on 'stagecraft'.

Stagecraft

When you're writing about a novel it's always productive to focus on narration. Narration includes narrative perspective, such as first and third person, types of narrator, such as naïve and unreliable, as well as narrative techniques, such as the use of dialogue, cross-cuts and flashbacks. Narration is worth focusing your attention on because it's an absolutely integral feature of all novels and short stories. In plays the equivalent of narration is called stagecraft. Examining stagecraft is an incisive and revealing way to see the writer at work. Some playwrights are able to use all the craft and resources of the theatre, namely set, props, costumes, lighting and music, while for various reasons [technical, artistic, budgetary] other playwrights may be more restricted.

Shakespeare, for instance, doesn't really use lighting in his plays, except notably in *The Winter's Tale*, because most of his plays were performed at the Globe theatre and in daylight. His instructions on costume are also very limited, usually embedded within the texts, rather than stated separately in stage directions. Think, for example, of Malvolio's yellow cross-gartered stockings or Hamlet's inky suit of woe. On the other hand, the importance of costumes is underlined repeatedly in Shakespeare's plays by characters who disguise themselves by changing their clothes. For instance, Viola becoming Cesario in *Twelfth Night* or Kent and Edmund disguising themselves in *King Lear*. Repeatedly too, villainy in Shakespeare's plays tries to remain hidden under a layer of fine clothes.

The general sparsity of information about costumes has, however, allowed directors over the years to relocate Shakespeare's plays to all sorts of settings with a huge variety of matching costumes. In a recent RSC production of *Antony and Cleopatra*, for instance, the designs for the Egyptian queen's costumes were inspired by powerful contemporary female celebrities such as Beyoncé.

When a playwright is restricted in the range of stagecraft he or she can utilise, not only do the devices they do use become more prominent, but other integral aspects of stage business become more significant. As you will see when we turn our attention to Shakespeare's plays in later books in this series, but also here in *An Inspector Calls*, exits and entrances are always particularly important. The managing of exits and entrances is at the core of all plays. Exits facilitate changes in costume and allow actors to recover from or prepare for major scenes. Tracking these seemingly simple instructions always reveals interesting and significant patterns, particularly in terms of which characters know what information at crucial points in the action.

Stage sets

As we mentioned in our discussion of the key differences between novels and plays, the latter invariably have fewer settings due to the fact that dramatic texts have to be physically realised in stage designs. And, as we also noted, changing from one elaborate stage set to another presents problems for directors and, potentially for the finances of a production. What sort of choices does a stage designer have to make when creating a set? Firstly, a lot depends on the nature of the play, as well as the playwright, the director and the budget. Some playwrights are very particular about the settings of their plays and describe them in great detail.

The American playwright Tennessee Williams, for instance, wrote particularly poetic stage directions, such as those that open his play *A Streetcar Named Desire*: 'First dark of an evening in May' and the 'sky is

a peculiarly tender blue, almost turquoise, which invests the scene with a kind of lyricism and gracefully attenuates the atmosphere of decay'. If that isn't enough to get a stage designer shake and scratch their head, Williams finishes with a synesthetic poetic flourish 'you can almost feel the warm breath of the brown river' that is even more challenging to realise on stage.

Other playwrights will sketch out far more minimalistic sets. Samuel Beckett in *Waiting for Godot*, for instance, describes the stage set in the sparest way possible, using just six simple words: 'A country road. A tree. Evening'. [Despite the skeletal detail, in production, Beckett was notoriously specific and exacting about how he wanted the stage to be arranged.]

Even if the playwright doesn't provide a great deal of information about the exact setting, a director is likely to have an overall concept for a play and insist, albeit to varying degrees, that the set design fit with this. If, for instance, a director wishes to bring out the contemporary political resonances of a play such as *Julius Caesar* she or he might dress the characters like well-known American politicians and set the play in a place looking a little like the modern White House.

Given free reign, a stage designer has to decide how realistic, fantastical, symbolic and/or expressionist their stage set will be. The attempt to represent what looks like the real world on stage, as if the audience are looking in through an invisible fourth wall, is called verisimilitude and is the equivalent of photographic realism in fine art.

In *An Inspector Calls* Priestley's opening directions suggest this sort of set. We are told that the setting for Act one will be 'the dining room of a fairly large suburban house' with 'good solid furniture of the period'. The 'general effect' of this dining-room is that it is 'substantial and heavily comfortable'.

Priestley goes on to discuss how a 'realistic' set might be constructed to incorporate the settings of other scenes, such as the 'fireplace' for Act

two and the 'small table with telephone on it' needed for Act three. Though the playwright advises that it may be easier to 'dispense with an ordinary realistic set' [because otherwise the dining table 'becomes a nuisance'] it is clear that Priestley is imagining a traditional theatre space with a proscenium arch stage.

As pictured below, a proscenium arch stage forms a rectangular screen or frame surrounded by the proscenium arch at its top and sides. At the start of a play with this kind of stage usually the curtain will rise as the action begins and fall at the interval, as it does in An Inspector Calls at the end of Act two. In effect, the curtain forms a fourth wall enclosing the  interior theatre box-shaped space and when it rises this fourth wall becomes invisible as the audience see inside the box.

An alternative way of staging a play is theatre in the round. In this kind of arrangement, the audience usually sits on all four sides of the acting space, although sometimes they can be arranged in a circle. The acting space becomes an island surrounded on all sides by the audience. Theatre in the round has several effects. In particular it forces the actors to move about so that all the audience see their faces at least some of the time. It can also create a sense of intimacy, as the audience is literally closer to the actors and there's no screen or frame to lend distance and make the experience similar to watching a film. From any angle the audience will also be able to see other audience members as well as the actors, in some ways bringing them into the world of the play. Finally, theatre in the round can generate claustrophobia, making it seem like the characters are trapped within the island of the acting space, surrounded by the audience.

What does the description of the Birlings' dining-room reveal about them? Think about your own house and what it reveals about your family. Or, more specifically, what do the interior spaces, such as your bedroom, tell the world about your family and you? If you're like most teenagers, probably it will signal to the world that tidiness is a value turned by adults into some kind of moral principle. But what about your posters, decorations, books, furniture, bed? The Birlings' house is 'fairly large' and 'suburban'. This implies that they are quite prosperous and that they are not metropolitans or country people. Just as Mr. Birling is a little 'provincial', his house is 'suburban' and the interior of the house further expresses the characters of the senior Birlings.

The 'good, solid' quality of the furniture reflects both Mr. Birling's wealth and his good, solid position in society. He is a 'sound'useful party man' who recently has been Lord Mayor. The 'general effect' of the furnishings, and of the Birlings themselves, 'is substantial and heavily comfortable'. Priestley emphasises this link by describing Mr. Birling as 'heavy-looking'. 'Solid', 'substantial', 'comfortable', 'heavy' are also adjectives that have positive but also negative connotations. The overall atmosphere may be 'comfortable', but it is not 'cosy and homelike'. In other words, the house lacks emotional warmth, like Mrs. Birling who the dramatist describes as a 'rather cold woman'.

In the long-running and celebrated production of the play directed by Stephen Daldry the stage design is more symbolic than realistic. Picking up subtextual clues about the Birling family and their privileged and insular world, the director makes these details explicit.

The idea that the Birlings live a sheltered life, removed from and above the concerns of ordinary, working class people is made tangible by presenting their house as a sort of over large dolls house raised on stilts above the stage floor. At the start of the play the house is entirely closed and the audience only hear the amused dialogue coming from within. But as the play progresses the house slowly opens up and at times the characters descend from their elevated position to interact on ground level with the Inspector who remains on the stage floor. The stage floor itself is obscured by mist. We won't give too much away about this ingenious design, just in case you haven't yet seen the production. Suffice it to say that as the Birlings lives and lies fall apart so too does their house.

Within the Birling house there's several rooms, one on stage and several off-stage: The action takes place in the dining-room, an appropriate place for a meal and a celebration, but when Birling decides he needs to speak man-to-man to Gerald, the female characters retire to a drawing-room. Characters leave the dining-room again towards the end of Act one – Mr. Birling leaves to inform Mrs. Birling about the Inspector's arrival and the Inspector also goes to the drawing-room after he has told Gerald and Sheila that Eva Smith changed her name to Daisy Renton. This off-stage room is useful as place to remove characters to and, along with the sounds of the front door and reference to Eric's bedroom, help create a sense of the Birling house as a three-dimensional space.

Exits and Entrances

When the play starts the Birlings and Gerald and Edna are already present on stage. After Birling has delivered his lecture in Act one, Mrs. Birling, Eric and Shelia leave the dining-room, creating a short, but revealing duologue between a boastful Mr. Birling and a sycophantic Gerald. Eric's re-entrance into the scene alters the comfy, mutually admiring dynamic, adding a degree of awkwardness and tension. The only character to make a major entrance, however, is the Inspector. Priestley's stage directions imply that his entrance is impressive – the ominous name, Inspector Goole, is announced first by Edna – and when he comes in the Inspector 'creates at once an impression of massiveness, solidity and purposefulness' [a rather difficult instruction for an actor to pull off]. At this point in the play, the female characters are not on stage. This allows the Inspector to focus on Mr. Birling and for Priestley to emphasise Eric and Gerald's contrasting reactions to Eva Smith's story: Gerald [to Birling], 'You couldn't have done anything else'; Eric, 'Why shouldn't they try for higher wages?' Sheila's re-entrance allows Priestley to make the Inspector repeat the key, shocking information about how Eva Smith died and to consolidate what we have just heard about Mr. Birling's role in her death.

At the end of Act one, the Inspector leaves the room with Eric, allowing Sheila to interrogate Gerald in private about his knowledge of Daisy Renton. After Sheila has discovered the truth, the 'door slowly opens and the Inspector appears'. At the start of Act two, Priestley has the Inspector stand at the door for a 'few moments', once again slowing the action down, creating a mini freeze frame effect and heightening the suspense before the Inspector 'comes forward, leaving door open behind him'. Mrs. Birling re-enters the fray in Act two and immediately sets about trying to intimidate the Inspector. Because she has not heard what her daughter Sheila has heard, tensions begin to open up between the two women. Mrs. Birling's lack of understanding of what has been going on also makes the revelation of Gerald's affair more dramatic:

Inspector: [Sharply turning on him] Mr. Croft, when did first get to know her?

An exclamation of surprise from Birling and Mrs. Birling.

After confessing his affair with Daisy Renton, Gerald leaves the house in Act two to 'walk about – for a while' to try to clear his head. Equally significant is Gerald's re-entrance into the play in Act three. Having had a bit of time away from the heat of the action, Gerald had been doing some thinking and comes to the dramatic conclusion that 'that man wasn't a police officer'. Continuing this line of thought, a little later Gerald also works out that there is 'no proof it was the same girl'.

Before his wife is interrogated about her role in a prominent local women's charity, Birling leaves the room to check on Eric's whereabouts. This is significant as it reminds us that Eric has been absent for the whole of Act two. Therefore he has not heard about his mother's vital role in refusing Eva/ Daisy charity, nor the revelation that she was pregnant. Only after this shocking revelation, and after Sheila has realised and belatedly her parents also realise that Eric may be the young man in question, and after Mrs. Birling has expressed her strong opinion that the father of the child 'ought to be dealt with very severely' does Eric return.

Once again, with a device familiar from crime and horror films, Priestley uses the door to create tension and build expectation. This time, the Inspector 'holds up a hand' to signal quiet and concentrate all  of our attention on this precise moment. Then 'we hear the front door' before we see anything. Then, by turning toward the door, all the characters focus our gaze on this part of the set. And then they and we all 'wait, looking towards door', as if for some sort of symbolic revelation or dramatic entrance. Finally, Eric enters, 'looking extremely pale and distressed'.

Birling judges his son's story to be so traumatic and sordid that he insists his wife and daughter leave, 'Sheila, take your mother along to the drawing-room'. However, neither can bear to remain there and re-enter the scene just after Eric has confessed to stealing money from the Birling company.

Of course, one of the most dramatic exits is the Inspector's. After delivering his powerful and prescient closing speech about learning in 'fire and blood and anguish', he 'walks straight out' without looking at any of them or saying another word. The Birlings are left 'staring, subdued and wondering' and Shelia is 'quietly crying' before the front door slams again.

When Sheila becomes appalled by her parents' and Gerald's behaviour she 'moves towards' the same 'door', as if literally trying to escape from a world that now seems to her like a gilded prison.

Props

Props can, of course, be used in all manner of ways. In Arthur Miller's *The Crucible* at the climax of the play the protagonist, John Proctor signs a false confession of having committed witchcraft on a piece of paper. But when he is asked to give up this paper by the court officials he will not and his final defiance is shown dramatically when he tears this prop in half. In Shakespeare's tragedy *King Lear*, the physical ring of the crown is an emblem of the impossibility of splitting the kingdom successfully between Lear's daughters and therefore of the foolishness of the king's plan. In many of Shakespeare's plays props in the form of physical letters are intercepted and fall dangerously into the wrong hands, moving on the plot. Props can also be used as signals of character - heroes in Shakespeare's plays invariably brandish swords, while fops carry nosegays and villains hide bottles of poison. Props can be used to heighten a dramatic effect and, as in the example from *The Crucible* to tell in a single image or action something it would take words longer to do.

Before you read the next section list all the props you can remember appearing in the play. Try to arrange them in chronological order. Then write next to each one how they are used by the dramatist.

- Desert plates, champagne flutes
- Decanter of port
- Cigar box and cigarettes, cigars and cigarettes
- Port glasses.

Champagne, port and cigars are all luxuries and are associated with indulgence. Hence these objects indicate that the Birlings are having a celebration, that they are middle, or perhaps upper-middle class, and that they are wealthy. As a marker of social class and status, it's important to Mr. Birling that he tells Gerald that the port is 'exactly the same' as the stuff Gerald's father drinks. Quite clearly Mr. Birling is in control of the distribution of the port, cigars and cigarettes, indicating that, as host and senior member of the family, he is in charge of proceedings. So it is Mr. Birling who proposes a toast to the happy couple and raises his glass. However, as the first scene progresses he allows both Gerald and Eric to help themselves to the port. While this could be viewed as lacking social grace, carelessness or as relaxed generosity, more importantly it creates an opportunity for a director

 and/or actor to emphasise Eric's drink problem by pouring himself a large shot. This action also suggests Mr. Birling's obliviousness to his son's restless unhappiness and the problem drinking that is both a consequence and cause of this. The decanter prop is used more explicitly in this way at the start of Act three, when the stage directions tell us Eric 'goes for a whisky' and that 'his whole manner of handling the decanter and then the drink show his familiarity with quick heavy drinking'.

Who does what with which prop is also important: Edna, the maid, clears away the first props from the table, showing she is a menial and that this sort of work is beneath the Birlings. Indeed, it is also almost beneath their notice. Edna's work is nearly invisible to them, taking place with little comment and without any thanks; a little piece of stage action that neatly manifests the Birlings' lack of appreciation of, and obliviousness to, working people.

- The ring case & ring 'a beauty'.

Gerald produces the ring with a dramatic, romantic flourish just after the toast in Act one. Sheila and her mother react with great excitement. However, Sheila hands the ring back to Gerald after the revelation of his affair with Daisy Renton in Act two. Towards the end of the play, having he thinks exposed the Inspector as a fraud, Gerald offers the ring back to Sheila: 'Everything's all right now, Sheila [holds up the ring.] What about this ring?'. In fact, Mr. Birling has just encouraged his daughter to ask Gerald to give her 'that ring you gave back to him'. It's significant that not only does Sheila ignore her father's unsubtle promptings, but she also rejects Gerald's offer. Hence the ring and attitudes to it economically conveys the changing dynamics of Sheila and Gerald's relationship.

- The Inspector's photograph
- A light – 'perhaps standard lamp'
- The tantalus on the sideboard.

The revealing and the not-revealing of the photograph is, of course, a crucial piece of stage action. Once it is clear that the Inspector will show the photograph only to one character at a time it becomes a source of mystery, tension and suspense. When the Inspector first shows the photograph to Birling, for instance, Gerald is irked that he is excluded and responds tetchily. The second time Inspector Goole produces the photograph he shows it to Sheila. The effect is immediate and dramatic: 'She looks at it closely, recognizes it with a little cry, gives a half-stifled sob and then runs out'. Meanwhile the 'other three stare in amazement for a moment'. Immediately afterwards Birling demands angrily, 'What the devil do you want to go upsetting the child like that?' and both Gerald and Eric exchange terse words with the Inspector. When the photograph is shown for a final time, to Mrs. Birling, she at first denies that she recognises the image:

Inspector: [taking back the photograph] You recognise her?
Mrs. Birling: No. Why should I?

This leads to Inspector Goole directly accusing her of lying: 'You're not telling me the truth'. And despite her initial denial and reluctance to do so, eventually Mrs. Birling has to reveal that she did recognise Eva/ Daisy and, in fact, had seen her only a fortnight ago.

A tantalus is a wooden box in which spirits such as whisky are kept. When he is shaken by the mention of Daisy Renton, Gerald goes over to the tantalus to pour himself a drink, in order to steady his nerves. Both Eric and Mr. Birling do the same thing later in the play. As we've already noted, Eric helps himself to a whisky at the start of Act three, 'his whole manner of handling the decanter and then the drink' revealing his 'familiarity with heavy drinking' and Birling 'pours himself out a drink' immediately following Inspector Goole's departure, again in attempt to regain his composure. Birling and Gerald take another drink once they have figured out that they may have been hoaxed. Clearly, then, alcohol plays an important role in the Birlings' life and some of their hysteria and irascibility is fuelled by the regular drinking that occurs throughout the action. In marked contrast, Inspector Goole refuses Mr. Birling's offer of a whisky and remains throughout the action entirely sober and unerringly serious.

- A chair.

There's a chair: Mrs. Birling 'collapses' into it after the Inspector leaves. Physically this conveys her exhaustion, but also diminishes her stature. Like the sideboard, the chair could be classified either as a prop or part of the stage set. A set designer needs to be attentive to this detail, otherwise Mrs. Birling will have nothing to collapse into.

- The telephone.

Used first after Gerald's re-entrance into the play to check on the existence of Inspector Goole, the telephone is a very effective stage prop. The second time it's used is to check whether any girl has been admitted to Brumley hospital having committed suicide by drinking disinfectant'. The pause while Mr. Birling waits for the answer, and the fact that neither the other characters nor the audience can hear what the other person is telling Mr. Birling, generates great intrigue and tension; 'Birling wipes his brow, Sheila shivers, Eric clasps and unclasps his hand'.

The telephone is also used to create tension in the last moments of the play when, in the middle of Birling's chirpy dialogue, it 'rings sharply'. The sense of shock is registered in a 'moment's complete silence'. Like the ring of the door, neither the onstage characters nor the audience

 know what this phone call might mean. As before, we all wait with hushed, baited-breath, trying to work out from Mr. Birling's fragmented half of the phone conversation what is actually being said: Mr. Birling: 'Yes? ... Mr. Birling speaking... What? – here – '

Ellipses and hyphens are used to indicate pauses and convey Birling's difficulty in processing the information. We'll return to this moment a little later, when we focus on the use of ambient sounds in the play.

Costumes

Fashion changes all the time and those of you with a keen eye for fashion will be able to spot what is in fashion and what's not each season. Different social groups also have associated fashions and these associations change over time. Think of the Doctor Marten boot, for instance, or pairs of Nike Air trainers. Costumes also suggest the age of characters and their social background. Think of a tweed jacket, for instance, or a pair of ripped dungarees. In Shakespeare's time the sumptuary laws were still in place. These laws dictated what people could and could not wear depending on their status in society.

As we've mentioned already, some playwrights are very specific about costumes, while others are happy for directors, actors and designers to make their own choices. At the start of the play, Priestley tells us that the Birlings and Gerald are 'in evening dress of the period,' with 'the

 men in tails and white ties, not dinner-jackets'. What precisely the ladies are wearing is left for others to decide, but we can imagine it will be fairly ornate and expensive. A little research would help a costume designer to choose costumes that are likely to establish a difference between Mrs. Birling's dress sense and her daughter's probably more modern style. We also learn from the stage directions that the Inspector is 'a man in his fifties', 'dressed in a plain darkish suit of the period'. The adjective 'plain' fits the Inspector's strikingly direct style of talking and his ordinary, man-of-the-people working attire establishes a sharp contrast with the dressed-up, wealthy and over-privileged Birlings.

Lighting

Lighting can be used starkly and boldly, such as in picking out a main character in a bright spotlight, or it can be used more subtly to convey mood and generate atmosphere. Intense white light makes everything look stark. Blue lights help to create a sense of coolness, whereas yellows, oranges and reds generate a sense of warmth and even passion. Floor lights can light an actor from beneath, making them look powerful and threatening. Light coming down on them from above can make an actor look vulnerable and threatened, or even angelic. Changes of lighting between scenes are common ways of changing the pervasive atmosphere.

At the start of Act one Priestley is quite specific about the lighting: It 'should be pink and intimate'. This lighting suits the domestic scene and the romantic occasion being celebrated. There is only one other lighting instruction in the entire play: when the Inspector enters the lighting should be 'brighter and harder'. Clearly the intention is to dispel the earlier intimate atmosphere and change the dynamic. Light brightening is associated with things being revealed and bright light can be harsh, while 'harder' light suggests an all-together tougher atmosphere appropriate for the Inspector's interrogation of the 'suspects'.

Music & sound effects

Music is, of course, a highly effective device for developing mood and atmosphere. In Arthur Miller's play, *A View from the Bridge*, for instance, a romantic popular song, 'Paper-Doll' is played while two young lovers dance together in front of a man who absolutely detests and opposes their relationship, and a charged, threatening atmosphere is immediately generated. In another of Miller's plays, *Death of a Salesman* a flute is used as a leitmotiv for the dreaminess of the central character Willy Loman. Though Priestley doesn't use music, off-stage sound effects feature significantly in *An Inspector Calls*.

As with the references to off-stage rooms, these ambient sound effects help generate a three-dimensional representation of the Birlings' house. Used sparingly, at various moments of the play, sounds from off-stage also immediately create tension. For instance, Mr. Birling's speech in Act one about how a 'man has to mind his own business' is interrupted suddenly and, of course, significantly, when 'we hear the *sharp ring* of a front door bell' [our italics]. The adjective 'sharp' is important, as it implies that the noise is sudden and shrill, but also that it cuts through Mr. Birling's bombastic blustering.

There are several references to the front door of the Birling house being opened or closed. When Gerald leaves in Act two, 'we hear the front door *slam*' [our italics]. Soon after 'we hear the front door slam again' and the audience is unsure whether Gerald has returned early or whether Eric has left the house for an unknown reason. What we do know is that the door has been closed violently. We also 'hear the front door' before Eric re-enters the dining room at the end of Act two and it 'slams' yet again after the Inspector leaves in Act three.

In Act three there is another sudden 'ring at the front door', frightening all the Birlings, ['They look at each other in alarm']. The Inspector has recently left, and Shelia and Mr. Birling have begun wondering whether the man who visited them was a real police inspector. For the elder Birlings this line of thought leads them to thinking about how they might be able to cover up their behaviour. Once again it is Mr. Birling who is interrupted by the doorbell. Their alarmed reaction to this sound suggests fear and guilt. Like them, the audience do not know whether the Inspector may have returned, or whether the doorbell has been rung by Gerald. Another moment of suspense is generated.

At the very end of the play, the 'telephone rings sharply'. Once again the sound cuts through and immediately transforms the atmosphere on stage. At this point in proceedings, Mr. and Mrs. Birling are almost hysterical, giddy with relief, and are laughing at the appalled reaction of their children. Once again it is Mr. Birling who is interrupted, just as he is accusing his children of not being able to 'take a joke'. As there have already been two phone calls in the final scene, one to the police station and the other to the hospital, the audience can guess that this one will also convey some crucial information. The Birlings' reaction to this sound implies that they too come to the same conclusion: 'There is a moment's complete silence'. Silence, like the stillness at the end of Act two, when the Inspector 'holds up a hand', creates dramatic anticipation. Silence is a space waiting to be filled.

Proxemics

Proxemics is the study of interactional body language and personal space and their significance in human relations. In Theatre Studies it's used to explore how characters occupy the stage space and how character relationships are depicted. For example, simple power dynamics can be indicated by characters standing up or sitting down and allegiances by how characters either group together or separate themselves from others. Similarly, using the stage space, a director can focus our attention on a character by placing them centrally and downstage closer to the audience, or do the reverse, hiding them in the background of a scene. Sometimes a playwright will be specific about proxemics, at other times directors and actors will work these out during rehearsals, picking up embedded clues in the text, as we'll go on to illustrate. Part of the challenge of reading a play for a reader is picking up non-verbal forms of communication that allow us to fill in the crucial visual dimension to the action.

No doubt, there'll be some attention on proxemics in our character essays, so at this point, we'll restrict ourselves to just a few observations about moments in the play when the proxemics are important. At the  start of *An Inspector Calls*, for example, Priestley is specific about who is sitting where around the table. As hosts, Mr. and Mrs. Birling sit at each end, with Eric on one side and Sheila and Gerald on the other. The senior Birlings' authority over the children arranged between them is thus immediately signalled. Another sign of Mrs. Birling's status, and of the importance of middle-class etiquette to the Birlings, is that when she rises from her the dinner table the other characters also rise. In contrast, when Edna enters with news that the Inspector has arrived the men do not rise from their sitting position. Priestley doesn't specify where the Inspector sits when he is invited to by Mr. Birling, but directors will be tempted to place the Inspector somehow pointedly apart from the others. In the Stephen Daldry production we've already mentioned, the Inspector remains outside the house, at ground level, while Mr. Birling descends only partly down a spiral staircase from the elevated house to address him.

Examples of embedded stage directions that imply proxemics appear at the end of Act one. At this point in the play, the Inspector has just revealed that Eva changed her name to Daisy Renton, eliciting a startled 'what?' from Gerald. Then Goole and Eric exit the room, leaving the newly engaged couple, Gerald and Shelia, alone on stage for the first time. What follows is a tense, awkward conversation, especially so for Gerald. Both characters are aware of an emotional gap suddenly opening up between them as they begin to see each other in a new light, and, sensing this, Gerald physically tries to bridge this gap. The stage direction says 'approaching her' and his line 'Now listen, darling - ' is left dangling uselessly in mid-air. Sheila responds tersely and firmly: 'No, that's no use.' If you were the director how would you position the actors during this exchange?

Certainly, the fact that Gerald has to 'approach' Sheila implies they are standing physically apart. What gesture might Gerald make as he approaches Sheila? Does he hold out his hands, palms upwards as he moves? Does he try to put his arms around her? That his line of speech is cut off also implies his movements might be arrested to. How does Sheila react physically? Does she recoil, move further away from him, cross her arm perhaps? Priestley's stage directions signal that when Sheila fires questions at him Gerald remains silent and still and does not dare look at her. A pause is indicated by 'he does not reply' and only near the end of her speech does it say he 'does not reply but looks at her'. After that no mention is made of either of their movements, suggesting the actors should stay static in the same,  fixed position, physically apart from each other, until the 'door slowly opens' and the Inspector reappears.

Generally there's not a great deal of dramatic physical action in *An Inspector Calls*. Mostly the play is driven forward by dialogue, with the characters occupying fixed positions, such as sitting at a table or on a chair. However, in Act three, when the Inspector reveals to Eric that Eva/Daisy had gone to his mother's charity to plead for help and tragically had been turned away, Eric is driven nearly wild with grief and rage: 'Then – you killed her. She came to you to protect me – and your turned her away – yes, and you killed her...' Although Priestley doesn't use a stage direction to tell the actor to physically get up and threaten Mrs. Birling, the reactions of the other characters function as embedded stage directions:

Sheila: [frightened] Eric, don't – don't –
Birling: [furious, intervening] Why, you hysterical young fool – get back – or I'll –

Birling's lines suggest he might be physically struggling to hold Eric back. Indeed, in some productions, Eric picks up an object, such as the whisky bottle, and looks for a moment like he might smash it down on his mother's head. In this context of sudden, violent movement, the Inspector's command to 'stop' is made even more powerful.

When Mrs. Birling collapses into the chair the stage designer has assiduously remembered to place on stage for that purpose, the action manifests the Birlings' exhaustion and defeat. However, when Gerald Croft re-enters the house and begins to raise profound questions about what we have just witnessed in Act three, everyone becomes gradually more animated. Mr. Birling, in particular, rediscovers some energy. There are noticeably more stage directions signalling movement at the climax of this scene – Birling 'goes to the telephone' and then goes to the sideboard; Birling raises his glass; Birling points at his children; Sheila moves towards the door, Gerald holds up the ring. Combining with stage directions that stress a huge shift in tone, such as 'heartily', 'jovially', 'amused' and 'triumphantly', these physical movements help convey a growing sense of energy, excitement – an almost giddy release of tension. The final scene's febrile energy builds to a small crescendo before the telephone's sharp ring and the following moment of 'complete silence' brings it to a crashing stop.

Dialogue & conversational analysis

Conversational analysis is a branch of discourse analysis used in linguistics to analyse patterns of meaning-making in human conversation. Although conversational analysis is conventionally applied to real conversations between real people in the real world, it can be easily and usefully applied to literary texts, especially to dialogue in novels and plays. Conversational analysis makes explicit the significance of underlying features of everyday conversational behaviour, such as variations in the length of contributions by speakers, modes of address and politeness terms, topic control and relevance, turn-taking, interruptions, asking and answering questions and truth telling. Often conversational analysis brings to our attention sub-textual issues of power and status between interlocutors.

Think, for example, of a situation where the power and status relationships are explicit and obvious, such as a classroom. If you were to read a transcript of a lesson, how would you know that the teacher was in control, presuming the teacher was in control? Firstly, of all the potential speakers in the class, probably the teacher will speak the most and with fewest interruptions from others. Secondly, the teacher will probably speak first and last, opening and closing the discourse. We would also expect that the teacher to be in control of the topic and to set the agenda of any discussions and that she or he would ask questions that the pupils are expected to answer. In a situation where the teacher asks something like 'so how many people read Act 3 for homework as asked?' and a pupil answers with something like, 'I ate all the bananas, because I really like bananas' we can readily see this isn't the appropriate response and the teacher's authority may be being challenged.

So, bearing this in mind, let's look briefly at a short section from the opening of the play. Mr. Birling is the first to speak and he dominates the conversation for the first few pages, speaking far more lines than any other character. He also sets the topic and controls the agenda of the conversation, firstly by proposing a toast to Gerald and Sheila and secondly by offering his thoughts on the current state of the world. He's deferred to by the highest-status character present, Gerald Croft, who responds eagerly to Birling's unsubtle prompts for approbation, chips into the conversation only when prompted and addresses Birling as 'sir'. Birling holds forth, sometimes at considerable length, in effect, overstepping his 'turn' and hogging the conversation. He is also the one who asks questions – 'Giving us the port, Edna?'; 'Special occasion, y'know, eh?'; 'Are you listening, Sheila?'. Moreover, he is able both to interrupt his wife without any reproach and also to brush aside other characters' attempts to interrupt him, such as his son's and later his wife's:

Eric: Yes, I know – but still –
Birling: Just let me finish, Eric.
Mrs. Birling: Arthur!

As Mrs. Birling shows signs of interrupting

Birling: Yes, my dear, I know – I'm talking to much. But…

When the Inspector arrives, Birling initially continues in this dominant role, issuing commands, such as 'Sit down, Inspector', again takes the lead in the conversation and asks a series of questions – 'Well, what can I do for you? Some trouble about a warrant?' Noticeably the Inspector and Birling address each other and neither Eric or Gerald are involved at all in the discussion, emphasising their secondary importance. Very quickly the power dynamic shifts however. After only a few exchanges, or conversational turns, the Inspector forcefully interrupts Birling '[cutting through, massively]' and completely ignores what he was saying. From then on, the Inspector takes full control of the conversation and soon becomes the character asking all the others questions, questions that they have no choice but to answer.

Of course, we could continue with this sort of conversational analysis, focusing on each character in turn, but as the opening scene is covered in one of our extended essays we'll leave it at that for now. In this example most of what is revealed through conversational analysis is little different from what might be gleaned through conventional literary analysis. This is because, at this point in the play, Priestley is not being terribly subtle in his portrayal of the characters and their relationship. At other times in plays, and in this play, conversational analysis may be able to reveal what is going on subtextually, i.e. underneath the words the characters are saying. Hence we'll draw on this approach from time to time when we analyse other scenes from the play.

The nature of the play

The whodunnit

From a thematic point of view *An Inspector Calls* is really a political play. It stages a debate, albeit a somewhat loaded one, about political ideology, with the Birlings representing conservative individualism and the Inspector socialist collectivism. The style and genre of the play, the whodunnit or detective story, is the sugar-coating that makes the serious political content slip down more easily. A few spoonfuls of intrigue and suspense ensure that the ideological matter is a little more palatable. At the time of writing, detective stories, such as those written by Agatha Christie, were popular on the stage and in the cinema, so Priestley uses the genre as a handy vehicle to express his political convictions in an entertaining way.

Priestley deviates from the conventional detective story a little. Usually this sort of story begins with the body of the murdered person being discovered. Then the Inspector arrives at the country house, or other helpfully enclosable space, and begins the methodical process of interrogating in turn the witnesses/ suspects. When writing the play, Priestley had several alternatives from which to choose: Why not have had Eva Smith murdered by one of the Birlings? Or perhaps by one of their stooges in order to silence her? Who, for instance, would ever suspect the quiet, dutifully unobtrusive Edna of being a cold-blooded contract killer? Knocking Eva Smith on the head with a candlestick after she'd visited Mrs. Birling and then dumping her weighted-down body at the bottom of a nearby lake, Edna would be the perfect killer. Clearly, as it is, the play veers dangerously close to melodrama, and while melodrama can be entertaining it tends to detract from a play's seriousness. And Priestley has a political message he wants the audience to take away from the play. Having Eva murdered would also push the bounds of credibility too far and turn the Birlings into a ruthless crime family, like a Brumley-based Sopranos. Isn't it important too that Eva kills herself? The fact that she committed suicide evinces her despair and therefore emphasises the cruel and heartless way she was treated. Whereas we would feel perhaps horror if she were murdered, we feel instead pity, sympathy and anger at the terrible waste of her life.

There are advantages and disadvantages to the use of the whodunnit formula. One advantage is that after Mr. Birling has been interrogated and we discover his role in Eva's death, the audience is able to anticipate how the events will unfold. Once Sheila has also been found culpable, we may be able to predict that somehow all the Birlings and Gerald are involved in Eva Smith's death and the fun will be in finding out how. As well as generating suspense and intrigue – how will each character be drawn into the narrative - this makes the structural pattern of the play comfortably familiar, as we move sequentially from one character being interrogated to the next. But this advantage can also be a disadvantage too. For 'comfortably familiar' read predictable. A series of interrogations, effectively a series of duologue with similar outcomes, creates very repetitive stage action. And the involvement of each character stretches the boundaries of probability to their limits.

What else does Priestley gain by clothing his rather didactic political play in the garb of a whodunnit? Firstly, it allows him to have a detective as a main character and secondly it facilitates a dramatic swerve at the end of the narrative, a twist in the tale.

Detectives are popular figures in narratives. Just look at the number of them currently scrambling about the place solving crimes on our TVs. The most famous detective of all, Sherlock Holmes, is among the most filmed characters in history. What makes a detective such an attractive  character for writers and audiences? No doubt we'll explore some of this topic in our essay on Inspector Goole, so for now, suffice it to say, that detectives are highly comforting figures, because they are able to resolve seemingly impossible mysteries and discover hidden truths. Cleverer and more perceptive than the rest of us mere mortals, they often embody the powers of rational intelligence. Perhaps Sherlock Holmes, Hercule Poirot and Miss Marple could look after themselves in a bare-knuckle scrap, but really their super-power is the unusual acuity of their minds. They are also figures of justice, dedicated to doing good in the world, unmasking criminality and ensuring it is suitably punished. Perceptive, articulate, always knowing more than the other characters, always ahead-of-the-game, Inspector Goole is certainly cut from this distinguished cloth. And, if this sort of dignified, good-doing, entirely reliable person – a priest-like truth-teller who is much cleverer than us - is a socialist, clearly then we should also be socialists too!

Whodunnits often end with a clever twist. All the signs were pointing emphatically to only one conclusion - that so-and-so must definitely be the murderer, when suddenly, with a stroke of genius the detective reveals that we were being misdirected by the master puppeteer, the true villain. Priestley's twist at the end of *An Inspector Calls* is as dramatic, but different in nature to the sort of convention outlined above. The phone call at the end of the play doesn't reveal new information about responsibility for Eva's death, rather it raises profound and troubling questions about both the nature of the Inspector and the sort of play we have been watching.

A well-made play?

You'd be forgiven for thinking that this is a phrase expressing approbation and admiration. Originally when the term was first coined in the nineteenth century it did, but over time, labelling a play 'well-made' came to be, at best, to damn it with faint praise and, at worst, to suggest it was dully and lifelessly mechanical.

The playwright George Bernard Shaw [1856-1950] was particularly scathing about well-made plays, seeing them as formulaic constructions following a set of simple instructions. Nowadays the term 'well-made play' is used almost entirely in the negative, pejorative sense.

A key feature of the 'well-made play' was its adherence to neo-classical notions of good construction derived from Aristotle. In particular these types of plays tended to observe the three Aristotelian unities of place, time and action. In other words, according to this principle a play should take place in one major setting, take place over the course of a short period, something akin to the real time the events depicted would actually take place and that there should only be one plot. Combined together these three unities would create focus and concentration. Immediately we can see that Priestley does indeed follow the three unities. The entire action of the play takes place in the Birling household, specifically the dining-room, the events occur in real time and the narrative is focused on one event, the death of Eva Smith.

Generally, well-made plays were realistic or naturalistic in style. Attempting verisimilitude, the world on stage was meant to look like the real world and feature events that might happen in the real world. Other common features of well-made plays included: The most important action taking place off-stage and before the play itself begins; hidden secrets or information known by some characters, but crucially not by others; the use of letters, notes or diaries to reveal new information; plot twists; the build-up of suspense to a climax during which all is revealed, and a happy resolution. Clearly Priestley follows many of elements of this formula in *An Inspector Calls*: The play takes place in a recognisably realistic setting; Eva's death has happened before the play begins; each character has hidden information about their own interactions with Eva; the Inspector has a crucial photo and refers to Eva's diary; suspense is built towards the climax of the play, when it is revealed that the Inspector wasn't, in fact, an Inspector and that no girl had, in fact, died from suicide that night in Brumley hospital. But then having strictly followed this familiar formula, springing a surprise on the audience, Priestley then does something entirely different.

Rather than resolving the play neatly and decisively, Priestley throws a curve ball, making the audience question what they have just witnessed, leaving everything still up in the air when the final curtain falls.

Medieval morality plays

Clearly as a play *An Inspector Calls* is something of a hybrid. As we've established, it has aspects of a didactic political drama, particularly in terms of content, but also of a whodunnit, particularly in terms of style

 and structure. It's also constructed following the convention of a well-made play, but then also deviates from this model. It could, indeed, be considered a supernatural play, if Goole is interpreted as some sort of a ghost sent from the future and it is sometimes classed as a 'dining-room' drama, as opposed to a 'kitchen-sink' drama. On top of this, or perhaps more precisely beneath these layers, Priestley's play has aspects in common with medieval morality plays.

In these plays, the protagonist is an everyman figure [sometimes even called Everyman] who over the course of the dramatic action comes across a variety of other characters who embody universal vices, such as the seven deadly sins, as well as universal virtues, such as the four graces. During the play, the protagonist is tempted by the vices and fortified by the virtues so that they come to learn a particular moral lesson. Sometimes the plays also feature a character embodying justice or conscience. Clearly Eva Smith is a virtuous everyman, or everywoman, figure. It's difficult, however, for her to learn much during the course of the play, being dead at the start. The Inspector could be read as a personification of conscience or, indeed, of justice. That might help explain his rather otherworldly, even supernatural qualities as well as his desire to teach the Birlings a good stern moral lesson. And the Birlings themselves could be seen to be personifications of various vices. If so, who would you say represents which of the deadly vices?

Gluttony – lust – greed – pride – envy – wrath – sloth. Mr. Birling seems to embody several: greed, tick; gluttony, smaller tick; pride, tick. Mrs. Birling? Pride, surely. Sheila? Envy. Both Eric and Gerald could personify lust. Perhaps the moral scheme is less prescriptive than this; Gerald could also embody duplicity and the senior Birlings' biggest fault surely is their callousness. Mapping the medieval morality play too strictly onto the characters in *An Inspector Calls* would also deny them room for development. In these plays the secondary characters, the virtues and vices, are not transformed by the action; they are fixed, static characters. While the same could be said of Mr. and Mrs. Birling and of Gerald, both Sheila and Eric learn from their experiences and become better, more likeable and more sympathetic characters as a consequence. So, as with the whodunnit element, Priestley draws on the medieval morality play tradition, but also deviates from it significantly.

Political theatre: Ibsen, Shaw & Brecht

Superficially at least Priestley's plays appear to have far more in common with contemporary English playwrights such as Terence Rattigan [1911-1977] than they do with the work of the innovative Norwegian playwright Henrik Ibsen [1828-1906], the influential Irish playwright George Bernard Shaw [1856-1950] or the politically radical German playwright Bertolt Brecht. As we have outlined, An Inspector Calls, like Rattigan's work, has many of the common features of well-made plays. The middle-class English dining-room setting also aligns it with popular plays of the 1940s by contemporary writers such as Agatha Christie and Noel Coward. Moreover, Ibsen's work is suffused with poetic symbolism and, famously, Brecht utterly rejected realism. It's hard too to imagine the experimental Norwegian, the excoriating Irishman or the communist German playwright having much interest in the decidedly middle-brow genre of the whodunnit.

On the other hand, Ibsen built plays, such as *A Doll's House* [1879], upon the sturdy structure of the well-made play. In addition to his innovations in style and in the depth of the psychology of his characters, Ibsen added greater moral seriousness to plays; characteristically Ibsen's works tackle major moral and/ or social issues and force the audience to re-consider their social mores, assumptions and values. In plays such as *Mrs. Warren's Profession* [1893] and *Pygmalion* [1913], Shaw followed Ibsen's lead, writing powerfully eloquent plays attacking what he perceived to be fundamental prejudices and injustices in British society. Like Priestley, Shaw was a lifelong socialist and frequently attacked inequities of the British class system. A founding member of the Fabian society, like Priestley, Shaw was also as intensely active in politics as he was in the theatre. Of course, Shaw is specifically referenced in the play. Mr. Birling dismissively cites Shaw as a prime example of the sort of left-wing intellectual who were warning that society had to change.

Brecht's plays are more stylistically radical than either Ibsen's or Shaw's. The German playwright developed highly radical staging techniques, such as having actors sit on stage even when their  characters were not involved in a scene or opening up the whole stage so that the audience could see into the wings, in order to destroy the illusion of reality traditionally associated with the theatre. In essence, Brecht believed that the traditional popular theatre of his time was far too focused on idle entertainment and was, fundamentally, empty-headed, decadent and sickly. What it needed was a good strong dose of ideology. Audiences shouldn't go to the theatre to be entertained, to lose themselves in some foolish narrative, but rather to learn something useful about themselves and the state of the world.

As part of his rejection of traditional theatre technique, Brecht's characters tended towards stereotypes. Sometimes, indeed, the actors in his plays wore labels to inform the audience exactly what sort of stereotype their character represented. This links Brecht's plays back to medieval morality plays, and we could read Priestley's often rather broad characterisation and aesthetics in *An Inspector Calls* in this moral, politicised light. In other words, Priestley's play is fundamentally political and specifically socialist, and the other aspects, such as characterisation, are devised in order to persuade the audience to accept a particular world view. Hence conservative critics, can, and indeed do, dismiss *An Inspector Calls* as essentially agitprop - theatrical propaganda for communism or socialism. For less politicised readers, the issue of whether the play fails to really come to life and falls short of literary greatness due to its political biases remains open for debate.

The playwright

According to the contemporary novelist, Graham Greene, through his radio programmes during WWII, J. B. Priestley became to the British public 'a leader second only in importance to Churchill'. Indeed, these programmes are widely credited with helping to strengthen public morale during the war. Estimates suggest that at this time around 40% of the entire adult population of England tuned in to Priestley's programmes. Not a bad effort for a lad from Bradford who left school at sixteen.

After leaving school and working as a clerk, Priestley had joined the British Army in 1914 and was badly wounded in 1916 when he was buried alive by a trench mortar. Once the war was over he took at degree in Modern History and Political Science at Cambridge University. His interests in history and politics were not limited to the theoretical and artistic; as well as being credited with influencing the establishment of the Welfare State, Priestley co-founded the socialist Common Wealth Party [CWP] and the longer-lasting Campaign for

Nuclear Disarmament [CND]. Always interested in the social conditions in England, at the height, or perhaps depth, of the Great Depression, he travelled through the country, producing a travelogue in 1934 detailing his observations.

To call Priestley a playwright is to undervalue the range and scale of his interests and talents. First gaining attention as an essayist, then acclaim as a best-selling novelist, he came to playwrighting in the middle period of his literary career. At the same time, he was also working as a journalist, social commentator and political activist. A prodigious writer, during his career, Priestley wrote twenty-six novels and thirty-nine plays. According to Margaret Drabble, Priestley 'conspicuously cultivated various poses – of grumbling patriot, cosmopolitan Yorkshireman, professional amateur, cultured Philistine, reactionary Radical', and was a Man of Letters 'who remained nevertheless a spokesman for the common sense of the common man'.[2]

In 1977 Priestley was awarded the Order of Merit, an honour limited to only twenty-four 'living greats'. Not a bad effort for a lad from Bradford who left school at sixteen.

---

[2] *The Oxford Companion to English Literature,* p.788.

Critical commentaries on key scenes

1.   The opening – trouble brewing

The curtain is drawn back at the start of the play to reveal the 'intimate' dining-room of the Birlings. Immediately positioned almost as voyeurs on this private celebration, we are uninvited guests looking in on the Birlings' 'substantial and heavily comfortable' home. Priestley is careful to point out that the dining-room should have 'good, solid furniture of the period', but that the general effect should not be 'cosy' and 'homelike'. This mise-en-scene serves a dual purpose: firstly, the audience of 1945 must be transported back in time to 1912; secondly we must gain a sense of the familial 'status quo' - these are people who live together and perform their relative roles, but they do not inhabit a 'home'; the atmosphere is not one of warmth and love.

The proxemics of the characters helps the audience to establish this picture. Arthur and Sybil Birling are positioned at opposite ends of the table, taking up their roles as host and hostess as tradition dictates, but communicating a sense of separation nonetheless. Sheila and Gerald are placed together, hinting at the nature of their relationship. Eric is sitting alone, potentially isolated, downstage. Finally, Edna is working hard clearing the dessert plates and champagne glasses, ironically the character with the most action but the least like to gain the audience's attention. Her role as parlour maid would be outdated for all but the wealthiest households by 1945 and serves to remind us of the stark class divide of the Edwardian period. The props with which she interacts also highlight this divide; the empty dishes represent the luxurious excess of the Birlings, further reinforced by the 'decanter of port, cigar box and cigarettes' [details particularly significant for a 1945 audience accustomed to years of rationing]. The audience views this scene for a few moments, observing Edna going about her business before the 'main' action begins.

The first piece of dialogue is directed towards Edna as Birling rather patronisingly observes: 'Giving us the port, Edna? That's right.' If it was not already made apparent through the mise-en-scene 'of the period' costume and Edna's actions as the curtain is lifted, her subservient role and Mr. Birling's enjoyment of it is emphasised with this opening line. It is important to remember also that lines of this nature also operate as embedded stage directions, providing clarity to the actor as to the actions they should perform as particular lines are delivered. Birling goes on to rather pathetically reassure Gerald that the port is the same as the one his father orders, whilst at the same time 'push[ing] it towards ERIC', his own son. So much is conveyed to the audience in this opening speech, and the stark parallels between the Birlings and the Crofts are established.

Not only will a 1945 audience understand immediately that Birling's 'rather provincial' accent precludes him from aristocratic 'breeding', his reassurance to Gerald demonstrates that Birling is his prospective son-in-law's social inferior and desires both Gerald's approval and acceptance as well as that of his father, who is notably absent. Birling's attempt to involve Eric whilst talking to Gerald communicates his desire to bring him into the ritualistic consumption of alcohol, perhaps attempting to draw him up to Gerald's level. This is an action which carries greater significance once the audience understands more about Eric's drinking problem and the consequences it has; clearly he has been exposed to and encouraged to participate in drinking as a status symbol and social expectation.

Gerald's claim to not know 'much about' port would further serve to illustrate his social superiority. His accent and manner would reflect his 'well-bred young man-about-town' persona, and his lack of interest in the topic shows he has the casual air of someone with nothing to prove. Sheila then hammers home the divide between the families by reminding her father that he doesn't really know 'all about' port, whereas Gerald's father 'prides himself' on his judgement of it. Birling ignores her jibe at his pretensions and instead insists his wife takes part in the drinking too.

It becomes apparent why Birling has been so keen to ensure all glasses are filled - in typical patriarchal fashion, he wishes to propose a toast. It takes quite some time for him to get to that point, however, as his wife, another of his 'social superiors' reprimands him on his complimenting of the meal in Gerald's presence – the comment indicates both Birling's craven neediness for Gerald's approval and his social clumsiness in seeking this. This leads into a discussion of Gerald's position within the family. An awkward moment arises between him and Sheila as he claims to have been 'trying long enough' to become part of the family. Sheila fails to respond, even after a second prompting, her mother answering for her 'of course she does'. The awkwardness expands further as, 'half serious, half playful', Sheila reminds Gerald of 'last summer' when he 'never came near' her. It would be obvious to the audience at this point that the enigma surrounding Gerald's whereabouts during that period is unlikely to have been simply due to being 'busy at the works'. Such a cliched excuse is almost embarrassing. Clearly Sheila doesn't buy it: 'that's what you say'. Her mother, the more experienced matriarch, is more likely to understand exactly what Gerald is covering up. But rather than behaving as one might expect as a protective mother and prospective mother-in-law - joining Sheila in giving the slippery young man a hard time - she actually defends him with a rather sickening pacification of her daughter. Patronisingly, Mrs. Birling explains 'When you're married you'll realise that men with important work to do sometimes have to spend nearly all their time and energy on their business. You'll have to get used to that, just as I did.'

The great Russian playwright and short story writer Anthon Chekov advised his fellow writers that if they included a gun in the first scene of a play then this gun had better go off some time later in the story. In other words, Chekov is emphasising that any striking details included in a narrative must have a purpose. And in this way, Gerald's evasiveness about what he was doing hints at future plot developments that will be realised in Act two.

An enlightened female audience of 1945 is likely to have slightly more self-respect than Sheila is encouraged to have here by her mother. In 1912 there were only 587 divorces in the entire year; by 1945 it had risen to almost sixteen thousand, and the rate at which divorces were happening was rising exponentially, having doubled since 1940. Whilst it is impossible to attribute this to a single cause, clearly times were changing and Priestley was drawing the audience's attention to what a young woman entering into a marriage in 1912 was expected to put up with - not only by her husband but also by the rest of society. The fact they are not yet married is key. Sheila's family have been given the strongest of hints that their future son-in-law may be a philanderer, but choose to ignore this, explaining it away as the way things are and Sheila just has to 'get used' to it. Sheila's short, emphatic response is likely to warm the audience to her, and hints at the promise she represents for the next generation's female enlightenment: 'I don't believe I will'.

The seemingly random interjection of Eric's sudden 'guffaw' at this point demonstrates his inability to sit silently by and watch this obvious charade. Having had too much to drink, he appears rather foolish, but his non-sequiturs act adds to the growing unease which surrounds the dinner table. Eric goes on to reveal that Sheila's accusation that he is 'squiffy' is a rather tame example of the unsavoury 'expression[s]' she has 'picked up' - a further hint another person around the dinner table has aspects of their life they are keeping hidden.

Finally, Birling is allowed to give his speech, and the absence of Gerald's parents for his engagement party is confirmed. Whilst they are 'abroad', this certainly feels like a deliberate social snub, and hints at the Croft's potential unhappiness with the match. The sense of this social affront is reinforced by the manner in which both Mr. and Mrs. Birling protest their preference for a 'quiet' celebration, when their desire for the Croft's approval is obvious. Birling's speech continues in this incongruous vein as he declares this to be one of the 'happiest nights of [his] life'. Barely commenting on the qualities of his daughter or future son-in-law at all, instead he chooses to describe the business transaction which will now take place, and his pleasure at being joined with 'Crofts Limited', a company which is both 'older and bigger' than his own. Reading between the lines, this appears to be a marriage of convenience for both families. Through it Birling can navigate himself up the social ladder, first through his own marriage and now through his daughter's, while the Crofts receive the kind of cash-injection aristocratic families classically came to need during the Edwardian period.

2.   The Interrogations

The dining room in Priestley's *An Inspector Calls* serves as a space for the performance of power, and it is a space that displays the Birlings' middle-class and bourgeoise sensibilities. Edna, standing in for the Edwardian servant class, is confined to the maintenance of this space. Devoid of a significant familial or symbolic role, she opens doors, brings food, and generally regulates and sustains the performance of wealth and power that the dining room facilitates. It is then notable that the stage direction that opens act two describes the Inspector as 'at the door', a repeated motif in the play. Moreover, he 'leaves the door open'. Hence the cloistered, regulated and protected space of the bourgeoise dining room is opened up, with its border left unguarded. And, indeed, the Birlings will be forced to recognise the suffering beyond their own contained spaces. This point nicely sets up the central themes of the act:

the revelation of moral truth and the disruption and forced dismantling of Edwardian bourgeoise ideology. With each passing interrogation through this central act, one more account or narrative perspective of Eva's life is challenged, altered, and remade from the Inspector's perspective. Each character's analysis of their own behaviour is challenged and reinterpreted, forcing a confrontation with their own sins, a facing up to the reality of capitalist exploitation.

The scene opens with an interaction between Sheila and Gerald prior to Gerald's interrogation. The interaction exemplifies the cloistered, protected character of a bourgeoise and patriarchal world. Gerald's attempt to reassert the authority and the power of his gender, drawing on archetypes of female madness and hysteria, reveals his awareness of the coming revelation and interrogation. While Sheila begins to understand the revelatory function of the Inspector, declaring to Gerald 'you see? What did I tell you?', Gerald attempts to suppress her newly disruptive voice, describing her as having a 'long, exciting and tiring day' and having experienced 'about as much as she can stand'. His language infantilises Sheila, representing her in terms of female hysteria and weakness, directly contrasting his apparent sensibility and objectivity with her unstable emotionality. This constructed opposition serves only to delay or postpone his own psychological torment while his attempts to remove Sheila from the conversation symbolises his desire to suppress the truth about his relationship with both Eva, women, and the working-class. This subtle interaction between two voices, one increasingly radical, and one conservative and unchanged illustrates the central dynamic or dialectic of the interrogations. As his occupational name denotes, the Inspector's function is to uncover reality or truth beneath the performance of civility, to force a process of psychic introspection and new consciousness of the interrelationship between the political and the personal. This claim is further supported by the language of inevitability that Gerald uses only a little further down the page as he addresses Sheila: 'You've been through it - and now you want to see somebody else put through it'. His euphemistic use of the pronoun 'it' and the resignation within his voice express his sense that the process of traumatic revelation, instigated by the disruptive force of the Inspector, is inevitable. Gerald's childish protestations reveal only the futility of continued psychic repression, of attempting to endlessly ignore the reality of Edwardian capitalism and class-relations.

Over the next few lines the Inspector hints at another aspect or function of his role, that of the priest, absolving a flock who have sinned. Sheila's language throughout this passage is drawn from discourses of trauma and psychological disturbance; when the Inspector describes again the suicide she declares that she 'can't stop thinking about it' and the stage directions tell us she is 'distressed'. Sheila's language evokes the process of confession while the Inspector declares that 'you see, we have to share something. If there's nothing else, we'll have to share our guilt.' This conception of guilt as inevitable burden shared amongst all evokes Catholic doctrine and suggests this new aspect or function of the Inspector's interrogation; not only does he bring political truth and force personal introspection, he also facilitates confession, penitence and, potentially, absolution.

Gerald forms the next section of the interrogation and a more general focus is formed with regards to the indulgences of the male middle-class. This focus emerges with Gerald's eventual confession:

'Gerald: All right, if you must have it. I met her first, sometime in March last year, in the stalls bar at the Palace. I mean the Palace music hall here in Brumley.'

Sheila's response, in which she declares that they 'didn't think you meant Buckingham Palace', emphasises the sordidness of accepted male 'indiscretions'. Brumley Palace Music Hall comes to function as a space for the exercising of male desires, a space which facilitates private acts of indulgence that contrast sharply with the proper and civil performance of the dining or parlour room. Once more the interrogation leads to a confrontation of the true nature of bourgeois, Edwardian life: The Inspector forces the Birlings to confront the constant and yet concealed adultery that lies beneath the surface of their middle-class civility. This claim is further supported by Sybil's later and repeated declaration of the affair as 'disgusting', despite her previous claim that Sheila should tolerate the indiscretions of her partner and accept them as a necessary inevitability.

At this point Priestley introduces the figure of Joe Meggarty. We are informed by Gerald that Meggarty 'had wedged' Daisy Renton, as she is known at this point, 'into a corner with his fat carcass' with an intent to sexually harass her. Joe Meggarty exemplifies a sordidness concealed beneath supposedly respectable middle-class manners and status. As an 'alderman', Meggarty is a high-ranking council officer, yet he is characterised here by his physical unpleasantness and his normalising of sexual abuse of disempowered working-class women. Ironically enough, Gerald imagines himself as Eva/Daisy's liberator - her source of freedom from a vision of masculinity that he claims to deplore. As Sheila notes he perceives himself as the 'fairy prince' saving the princess from imprisonment, much in the mode of medieval, courtly Romance. However, what Priestley makes clear in his defamiliarising of this narrative pattern is that Meggarty's behaviour in fact mirrors Gerald's; they are two sides of the same coin. Gerald's claim that he does not 'install' Eva/Daisy as his 'mistress', a term imposed upon his actions by the Inspector, rings hollow. The verb 'install' makes painfully clear his perception of Daisy as part of the machinery of his own pleasurable existence, a tool or object on which to satiate his desires. Part of the revelation of this episode is the exposure of Gerald's similarity to Meggarty. Their apparent difference and opposition are shown to be artificial. It is only Gerald's youth, his attractive, aristocratic appearance that conceals the violent and coercive character of his sexual desires.

The process of Gerald's interrogation is characterised by two opposing forces or drives: Firstly, that of the Inspector and Sheila, who seek to uncover the true character of Gerald's actions in a ritual of confession; and secondly, that of the elder Birlings and, in part, Gerald himself, who seek to repress the truth of the affair, to conceal it beneath a superficial surface of etiquette and civility. As Gerald recalls his narrative, Birling interrupts early on 'angrily' declaring that he 'really must protest'. The qualifier 'really' and tone of righteous indignation employed here make clear that Birling's protestations stem from a desire to protect the good name of the Birling family. He goes on to note that there is no need to 'drag' Sheila, an 'unmarried woman', into this, despite her drive to uncover the truth and personal desire for reformation. His protestations are matched by those of his wife, who argues that they need not hear 'any further details of this disgusting affair'. Discourses of politeness and civilisation are revealed through these interruptions to try to conceal baser or more taboo behaviours. The accusation levelled at the Inspector by the elder Birlings is that his uncovering of this narrative is impolite; he challenges their bourgeoise authority in a manner that is, to them, simply morally unacceptable. Public morality is subverted – the respectable, according to the Birlings ought to be protected in their respectability as a matter of course, regardless of their actual behaviour.

This drive to further suppress problematic behaviours contrasts with Sheila's keenness to extract Gerald's confession. When Gerald acknowledges that he enjoyed Daisy's dependence on him, Sheila replies with praise, noting that it is 'probably the best thing you have said tonight. At least it's honest.' Sheila privileges confession and revelation here as process of purification or redemption. This is further emphasised by her breaking off of the engagement; the event is presented less as traumatic and more as transformative, marking a development that can only be positive:

'But this has made a difference. You and I aren't the same people who sat down to dinner here. We'd have to start all over again, getting to know each other—'

Sheila's reflection on how their relationship has changed makes clear their mutual and symbolic maturation - the re-organisation of personal identity that has occurred. The ambiguous difference here is emancipatory for Sheila, at least: She sheds a corrupt and patriarchal relationship, an act that precipitates the construction of a new, more egalitarian model of sexual partnership.

Sybil's interrogation follows much the same vein as the previous examples. The dialectical struggle between revelation and concealment established by Priestley throughout the second act continues. The question, for the purposes of our current topic, is how might Sybil's interrogation develop or iterate upon this established pattern or struggle between private and public selves, truth and performance? The answer, one might claim, lies in the deployment of a kind of shattering dramatic irony. As Sybil's account of rejecting a pregnant woman for charitable aid unfolds, the audience inevitably concludes that the formal patterning of the play necessitates Eric's guilt.

The interconnectedness, the repetitiveness of Priestley's plotting signals the coming revelation. Sybil, however, is, perhaps somewhat strangely, incapable of deducing this fact, declaring instead that the Inspector should 'go find the father of the child' as 'it is his responsibility'. Sybil places the blame on an imagined Other, a figure of worthless, sordid masculinity, no doubt of a class below her own, and yet, she is, of course, forced to realise this sin lies within her own family, her own world. Her dumb silence is all that is provided by Priestley to exemplify this moment of realisation, a dawning of truth, before the act is concluded. This disjunction between the audience or reader's knowledge and that of Sybil's no doubt emphasises her ignorance and myopia, but it also allows us to relish the dismantling of the Birling's existence, to stand above them as the Inspector reveals the structural operation of capitalism and patriarchy. This enjoyment, this schadenfreude, is central to the second act's progression, empowering the reader and audience to deny and mock the authority of individualist and capitalist philosophies.

3.   Eric learns the truth

First off, this is the best, most powerful, most dramatic, tensest scene in the play, isn't it? Up until this point in the play Eric has been rather in the background, either a quiet, rather nervous presence or entirely absent from previous scenes, supposedly resting in his bedroom. Both Mrs. Birling and Eric are going to discover new, unpalatable things about each other in this scene: The Birlings infantilise their children and are in denial about Eric's drinking problem and, crucially, Eric did not witness the previous scene when the Inspector questioned his mother about her role in Eva Smith's death. Therefore Eric does not know that the woman he had a relationship with, the woman he offered to marry and with whom he was going to have a child, came to his own mother, desperate for help, and was turned down, heartlessly. As Scene three begins, Priestley uses dramatic irony again, this time more deftly: We know all about Eva's visit to the Birlings' house, as do all the other characters on stage. Except for Eric, standing hesitantly 'just inside the room', stared at by all the others.

The previous scene has accelerated to a dramatic, explosive climax. It's a scene we have been anticipating almost since the start of the play where the two most formidable characters, the Inspector and Mrs. Birling finally come into open, almost bare-knuckled, conflict. Initially, in her customary formidable style Mrs. Birling has defended herself robustly, refusing to accept she has done anything wrong: 'I did nothing I'm ashamed of...I consider I did my duty'. In fact, initially, she throws the whole blame for the tragedy onto Eva herself: 'I'm very sorry. But I think she had only herself to blame'. Priestley skilfully implies throughout this interrogation that the Inspector is losing patience with the Birlings and is increasingly angered by Mrs. Birling's responses. In contrast to the more gentle, coaxing manner he adopted to question Sheila, with Mrs. Birling he is stern and to-the-point, sometimes flatly and bluntly contradicting her. The tension between the two escalates until the Inspector reveals a new terrible piece of information: 'this girl was going to have a child'. In response, Mrs. Birling takes a new tack. Now it's not simply Eva's fault that she found herself in a desperate situation: 'I'll tell you what I told her. Go and look for the father of the child. It's his responsibility'.

Quick, sharp exchanges of dialogue follow, increasing both the pace and the tension. Despite the Inspector's quick-fire questions and more and more details spilling out, Mrs. Birling continues to deny responsibility, 'I was perfectly justified in advising my committee not to allow her claim for assistance'. As this bruising, confrontational scene moves towards its climax, gradually the audience and Sheila piece things together, arriving at the truth before either of the senior Birlings. By then it is too late for Mrs. Birling. Steered and driven by the Inspector's relentless questions she concedes that if Eva had been telling the truth then the young man would be 'entirely responsible'. Despite Sheila's frantic attempts to interject, riding the wave of her indignation Mrs. Birling arrives at the conclusion that the young man must be 'compelled to confess in public his responsibility'. Only at the very end of the scene does the penny finally drop for her and for Mr Birling: 'She stops, and exchanges a frightened glance with her husband'; '[agitated] I don't believe it. I won't believe it…'

And then they wait, thunderstruck, dramatically looking towards the door. And then equally dramatically Eric enters, 'looking extremely pale and distressed'. And then, even more dramatically, 'the curtain falls quickly'. And the audience is made to wait for twenty minutes to discover what will happen next.

As the curtain rises again at the start of Act three, into this maelstrom enters Eric. Put yourself into Eric's callow shoes. Not only is he going to have to reveal his own shameful, sordid and, indeed, criminal behaviour to his sister, his parents and also to the Inspector, he's also going to discover that Eva's life could have been saved and that his own child could have been saved, and that it was his own mother who could have saved them and could easily have done so. That's an awful lot to swallow in one scene. Switch shoes, and step into Mrs. Birling's staunch pair. She is going to have her cherished illusions about her son violently torn to pieces. On top of that, she is going to have her own cruel and callous behaviour exposed. On top of that she will have to face her son's grief and outrage. Quite a difficult scene for her too then.

So, at the start of the scene things are already very tense with a lot at stake. Initially both Eric and Mrs. Birling speak tentatively and uncertainly. Uncharacteristically, Mrs. Birling's speech patterns are fragmentary, riddled with hesitations:

'But I didn't know it was you – I never dreamt. Besides you're not the type – you don't get drunk – '

By using hyphens and short, stuttering utterances, Priestley implies that Mrs. Birling is struggling to come to terms with what she is learning about her son. Perhaps too there is some suggestion of the dread she must feel at what will soon be revealed and how Eric might respond.

Meanwhile her son is acting like a condemned man. Stage directions convey his state of mind: He speaks 'bitterly' and 'miserably' and asks for a drink to steady his frayed nerves. And then the interrogation begins.

Noticeably Priestley gives the Inspector only very short, direct questions that help move Eric's narrative along - 'What did you meet her?'; 'Was she drunk too?'; 'When did you meet her again?' and so forth. Most of this part of the scene is a duologue, with the audience's attention entirely focused on the Inspector and Eric. Only occasionally are there interjections by other characters.

Eric's narrative quickly darkens and becomes disturbing. Reading between the lines, we realise that in her desperation Eva has been encouraged to try prostitution, 'There was some woman who wanted her to go' to the Palace Bar, a place that has already been established as the haunt of 'women of the town'. The following information about Eric's drunken behaviour is so shameful and distressing that he retreats into euphemistic ambiguity, unable to name explicitly what he did, 'And that's when it happened'. There is an implication that he may in fact have forced himself on Eva. The torture of confessing all this, out loud, to his family, is conveyed by Priestley again by using hyphens and short, broken sentence structures. In addition, Eric blasphemes,

'Oh – my – God!', Mrs. Birling cries out and Mr. Birling issues sharp commands. At this point, Sheila and her mother leave the dining-room to be spared the worst. Or so they think.

The conversation between the Inspector and Eric moves on quickly. We learn that Eva had told Mrs. Birling the truth and that Eric had stolen money from his father's business. Adding to the growing sense of disorder and tension, Sheila and Mrs. Birling re-enter, unable to bear not knowing what is happening. Up until this point, Eric has been entirely focused on admitting his own miserable behaviour, but then a new thought enters his head and the conversation takes a different, more dangerous turn.

The Inspector has established that Eva discovered the money Eric was giving her was stolen and so wouldn't take any more from him. Admitting this, Eric speaks in a 'sudden, startled tone: Here, but how did you know that?' If I were directing the scene, I'd try to stretch these excruciating moments as long as possible. The Inspector is blunt and factual and gives nothing away: 'No. She told me nothing. I never spoke to her'. Who's going to speak next? Are they going to tell him the truth? If so, who's going to tell Eric? Leave those questions lingering in the ether, hold this moment of intense suspense, before Sheila speaks up, quickly and directly, as if getting something dreadful off her chest: 'She told mother'.

Now Eric's mind works quickly. That means Eva must have come to his parents' house. Urgent questions spring up. Suddenly he is no longer being questioned, but becomes, instead, the questioner: 'She told you?… What happened?' If you were Mrs. Birling you might struggle to work out how best to answer your son's desperate questions. Again, another moment of terrifically tense silence, as she is unable or unwilling to respond: 'Mrs. Birling, distressed, shakes her head but does not reply'. But Eric is not going to let up now. 'Come on, don't look like that.' He shifts into the imperative and short sharp, insistent, desperate questions, 'Tell me – tell me – what happened?'.

Again, Mrs. Birling does not speak. Nor does Sheila, nor Mr. Birling. Imagine them on stage. What would their expressions be? At what are they looking? How and where might they stand? What would they be doing? The Inspector provides the answers, in typically stark, unforgiving terms: 'She went to your mother's committee for help, after she'd done with you. Your mother refused that help'.

As we mentioned in the earlier section on proxemics, what follows is a rare moment of physical action in the play. Almost crazed with rage and grief, Eric spits out short, angry phrases, 'Then – you killed her', obsessively repeating this brutal phrase three times, circling around it and coming back to the blunt accusation within a few lines. Priestley uses abrupt phrases to show Eric piecing things together, as if we are in his mind as he is having thoughts that hit him like physical blows, 'yes, and you killed her - and the child she'd have had too – my child – your own grandchild – you killed them both.' The speech ends with Eric cursing his mother, 'damn you, damn you -- ', and is followed by Mrs. Birling's 'very distressed' inarticulate denials. Eric's next lines are a splutter of accusatory rage. Sheila cries out with fear, afraid that Eric might physically attack their mother, 'Eric, don't – don't –', and, 'furious', Mr. Birling 'physically intervenes, 'why, you hysterical young fool – get back – or I'll –'. The flurry of hyphens at the ends of lines indicate that these lines should come hard upon each other in a dramatic device known as stichomythia. Priestley doesn't spell out any actions through stage directions here. We don't find out what Sheila doesn't want Eric to do, or what exactly it is that Birling is threatening to do to his son. These gaps leave space for directors to decide on the stage action. It is clear, however, that the emotions are running very high, that things have spun almost out of control and if there isn't any actual violence we on the very verge of it breaking out.

All this frenetic stage electricity is then halted by the Inspector, 'taking charge, masterfully' with a simple, commanding monosyllable. The effect, on the other characters and the audience, is immediate: 'They are suddenly quiet, staring at him'. Thus, Priestley brilliantly orchestrates the dynamics of this scene. Veering vertiginously from tremendous turbulence, violent action and fraught, shredded emotions everything comes crashing to a sudden, silent, shuddering stop.

4. The Phone Calls

The final act of *An Inspector Calls* is one of great structural interest. Typically, a parlour-room murder mystery quite nicely follows the Todorovian[3] narrative structure, and up until this point our play has done the same. We've experienced the classical opening which introduces us to the Birling equilibrium perfectly as they are poised around the dinner table. Then quite quickly tensions begin to simmer. The Inspector provides the conventional disruption to this situation, and we hear of our unfortunate victim, Eva Smith. A number of crises then unfold as the guilt of each of the characters is established, with the stakes rising higher and higher before the tension reaches its climactic point: Eric is the father of Eva's unborn child, and his own mother has had a hand in its death. As moments of high drama come, it's difficult to top that. The audience is likely to burst into a crescendo of chitter chatter as the curtain slowly closes on this revelation; cruelly the action is ripped away in a style later appropriated by soap operas with long-running success. The audience will now be expecting act three to provide the inevitable 'denouement'; a neat resolution to this

---

[3] Tzvetan Todorov was a narrative theorist, among other things. From studying fairy tales Todorov argued that narratives tended to follow the same pattern, from equilibrium via disruption back to equilibrium, as set out diagrammatically on the next page.

crises which neatly ties up any loose threads into a tidy bow so that they can go home satisfied with an evening's entertainment.

A Tension Graph for the 3 Act Structure

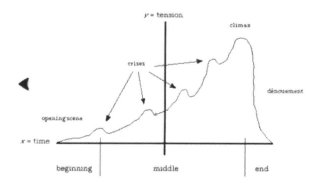

Initially it appears that this expectation will be fulfilled; Eric confesses his role in Eva's death and the final piece of the puzzle slots into place. Each character is guilty in a clever twist of the genre; a resolution similar to that used by Christie in *Murder on the Orient Express*, where each character took their turn with the knife. However, in Christie's narrative the victim was the truly guilty character, and his dispatchers were presented as just executioners. The antithetical reverse is true here; our victim is the embodiment of innocence - her own and that of her class. Our 'murderers' are the embodiment of guilt - their own and that of their class. This point is hammered home by the Inspector in what we could classify as his 'denouement' 'fire and blood and anguish' speech, aimed not just at the Birlings, of course, but also at the audience themselves.

A traditional parlour room murder mystery narrative would come to an end shortly after the dramatic 'reveal' of the detective; perhaps with the tying of a few loose ends, a side helping of some poetic justice followed by an anecdote involving the home life of the protagonist in which they dole out some philosophical wisdom. The audience will already appreciate that Priestley's narrative has deviated from the path they might have been expecting, nevertheless the exit of the Inspector has an air of finality about it; the ultimate resolution must surely not be far away now. It would be reasonable to expect the Birlings to take heed of those ominously prophetic words: 'fire', 'blood', 'anguish'. It would be reasonable to expect the play to end with the Birlings hastily discussing how they might make reparation for the harm they have unleashed upon Eva Smith and the 'millions and millions' of her counterparts in Brumley and beyond. Perhaps Birling will make a grand gesture towards his workers, providing them with fair wages and decent conditions. Perhaps Mrs Birling will vow to always treat those who come to her asking for aid without prejudice. Perhaps Gerald will return and resolve to treat Sheila faithfully for the rest of her life, and Sheila will turn him down because she has gained some respect for herself. As for Eric - does he hand himself over to the police for the manner in which he abused Eva, or vow never to drink again?

Of course, none of this transpires. In fact, the first person to speak after the Inspector makes his dramatic exit is Birling. And he opens his mouth to cast all responsibility away from himself and on to Eric: 'You're the one I blame for this'. We are then treated to a further dramatic spectacle in which a clear divide - or gulf - opens up between the Birlings and their children. The return of Gerald offers welcome respite from the rising tension, and the subsequent twist is revealed to Birling's sickening delight: the Inspector was not a real police inspector. The adverb 'excitedly' is used three times in quick succession to describe the manner in which Birling reacts to Gerald's news. Of course, both Sheila and Eric do not share in his delight, and the excitement soon turns to anger as they each maintain that their actions remain the same regardless of the 'Inspector's' identity. As Eric states: 'the girl's still dead and we all helped to kill her.' It's at this point that further genre reversals take place and we deviate entirely from our typical narrative structure: Gerald has already begun to take on the role of detective, and his mind continues to tick over the events as he questions whether or not they *did* all help to kill the girl. Birling now speaks 'eagerly' as Gerald unpicks the interrogation bit by bit, unthreading the loose ends at the point an audience might be expecting them to be tied together. Decisively he telephones the infirmary to discover that no young girl had been brought in that night.

This is the moment at which the Birlings are truly tested - and each one fails. Unsurprisingly, Birling smiles at them all and announces drinks all round. Gerald smiles back and gratefully accepts; Mrs Birling does the same and compliments Gerald on his cleverness - his 'disgusting' affair seemingly forgiven and forgotten. Sheila and Eric are the subject of Birling's ridicule, but react by resuming their argument with their parents. Not one of them reacts by asking the question: *How is Eva Smith right now*? Not one of them rushes to the door to attempt to track her down or to support her in what clearly would be her hour of need. They continue to behave as if she is some kind of abstract concept, to be mulled over and discussed. None of them thinks of her as a living breathing person who they can make a real difference to, then and there. It's true they each may have interacted with a different version of 'Eva', but it has been established that another member of the Birling family is on the way, and not one of them, not even Eric, suggests even the possibility that they try to make contact with her, either then or in the future.

Priestley places this test in their path for a number of reasons. Most notably he considered a number of time theories to hold moral value, and one interpretation of the play involves the application of these theories to the Inspector. Firstly, Ouspensky's theory centred around the idea that once we die we re-enter our life again from the beginning, with the same parents and living through the same events. This cycle would continue to repeat unless we learnt something significant and improved spiritually from one life to the next. If we are able to make significant spiritual improvements, the path opens for us to enter a new life in which we avoid making the same mistakes again and again. The Birlings are essentially offered the opportunity to break the cycle of their mistakes by the Inspector. He gives them a chance to make significant spiritual improvements. But, whilst Sheila and Eric go some way to learning from their mistakes, they still do not act upon the knowledge that is revealed to them, or show any intention of doing so in any practical sense.

A further theory of time which is discussed elsewhere in this guide is that of Dunne, who believed that you could be given the gist of seeing forward in time as well as looking back. You could therefore see what the consequences of your actions might be, and alter your actions to avoid those consequences if you wished. The Birlings are possibly given the opportunity to gain a glimpse of the future, but again, fail to change their behaviour in any meaningful way. This inaction results in the inevitable consequences; a further phone call reveals that a young girl has been taken to the infirmary and a police inspector is on his way. The cycle of events repeats itself as they fail to prevent it. The use of the telephone to deliver this information is again significant. Just as the doorbell provided the initial toll of judgement for Birling when the Inspector made his entrance, a second bell tolled [announcing Gerald's return] as Birling considered the course of action he would take as a result of the girl's death. A third bell now tolls piercingly into the room announcing the death knell of Eva, the death knell of the Birling's self-righteous position within society, and for the 1945 audience, the death knell of bourgeois class supremacy.

Critical essays on characters

The dangers of providing exemplar essays are that, inadvertently, they may close down your own thinking and encourage regurgitation of the essay's content in examinations. Our essays were not written in timed, examination conditions and are not examples of what an examination board would expect from you in those conditions. Hence, primarily, these essays are not designed as model answers; rather our aim is to provoke, stimulate and inform your own thinking about the play's major characters and make you reflect more critically on their roles and functions.

Hopefully, our essays will make you think again, perhaps even make you think differently. Sometimes you may also encounter readings with which you disagree. That's good; so long as you can explain and justify why you have come to different conclusions. Whether you mostly agree with their interpretations or not, these essays should, however, provide plenty of information you can digest, ponder, alter and then reformulate in your own words.

Remember when you are writing about characters to try to lift your perspective above the character-level action of who said what and who did what to the author-level perspective of why these words and actions are significant.

Mr. Birling

Priestley's caricaturesque portrait Birling is a damning one. Ignorant, exploitative, unrepentant - a capitalist sinner who perfectly fits the Marxist concept of a bourgeois parasite, gluttonously feeding off the toil of the proletariat, leaving them with a meagre subsistence and expecting them to be grateful for it. If they should complain? Woe betide them. It's Birling's 'duty' to keep 'labour costs down' of course - he is busy building a mighty nation impervious to the musings of socialist 'cranks' and the threat of war, a nation which builds 'unsinkable' ships and rewards dutiful citizens such as himself with knighthoods. He declares all of this within the first half of the first act, loudly and in his [potentially rather grating] portentous provincial accent. Significantly he manages to cover this diverse range of topics at his own daughter's engagement party, barely giving her a passing mention. Instead his toast is full of talk about the burgeoning business empire he will now preside over, alongside the aristocratic Crofts.

It is difficult to underestimate just how distasteful an audience in 1945 would have found Mr. Birling. A war-weary nation grieving several generations of loved ones and still subject to rationing, listening to a self-satisfied, ignorant and potentially fascist 'hard-headed' businessman reeling off one nonsensical diatribe after another would have been at best laughable. Once the tragic impact of his actions had been revealed and he is shown to be utterly unrepentant, it would have been sickening. Birling embodies everything distasteful about the nouveau-rich, a character trope well established within murder mystery fiction, particularly that of Agatha Christie. Juxtaposed with the well-bred manners of his 'social[lly] superior' wife and the smooth-as-you-like Gerald, Mr. Birling's character deviates, however, from the established trope.

Often in murder mystery narratives, the self-made-man stereotype ultimately reveals himself to be more genuine and down-to-earth than his blue-blooded counterparts. Not so for Mr. Birling. He may have a plain, 'tell it like it is' style, but he also has a habit of 'telling it like it isn't'. His ignorance is so profound and its consequences so catastrophic that any humour one might have felt at the distance by which he regularly misses the mark is turned sour. The 'absolutely unsinkable' Titanic resulted in the deaths of over fifteen hundred people, a metaphorical representation of both the arrogance of the British manufacturing industry who famously only supplied lifeboats for just over half the passengers, and the manner in which a hierarchical value was placed on the lives of the passengers dependent upon their class - sixty two percent of first class passengers survived compared to only twenty five percent of third class passengers. As a result of the inquiries held at the time, these tragic errors were well-documented, and many in the play's original audiences would have held the tragedy in living memory, given that it only took place in recent history for them.

Birling makes this proclamation as part of a lengthy speech he insists everyone listens to after the 'officiation' of Gerald and Sheila's engagement through the presentation of the ring. Once again, he makes brief reference to the marriage before he returns to his political agenda. He has several points he wishes to get off his chest, perhaps for the benefit of Gerald who he is keen to impress, and also for the benefit of Eric, who he is keen to influence and align to his point of view. Eric repeatedly attempts to interrupt his father with an alternative viewpoint - raising questions which with the benefit of historical hindsight the audience appreciate need examining. Dramatic irony lies heavily in the air as Birling gives a toe-curlingly inaccurate assessment of the political landscape, declaring 'pessimistic' fears of war 'silly talk' and 'fiddlesticks', and insisting they are marrying at a 'good time'. Rather sycophantically Gerald agrees, whilst Eric is scalded for appearing sceptical, perhaps reflecting the manner in which the younger generation are disregarded and shouted back into their place. On a personal level this has tragic consequences for Eric, with his marginalisation leading him to find solace in destructive places. For the younger generation as a whole in the Edwardian era, it had much more devastating and far-reaching consequences, as an audience thirty years on would have understood only too well. The dismissive manner in which Birling refers to 'the Kaiser mak[ing] a speech or two' and 'half-civilized folk in the Balkans' demonstrates the ethnocentric attitude which ultimately played a key factor in triggering the wars in the first place.

In case the ironic picture had not been drawn emphatically enough, Priestley hammers the point home with Birling's idealised vision of the future. He imagines Gerald and Sheila giving an engagement party for their own child, 'perhaps in the forties' when everyone will have 'forgotten all these Capital versus labour agitations and all these silly little war scares'. Again, it would almost be humorous if the stakes had not been so high, and the play verges into satire, with a sharply bitter edge. The lengthy speech Birling subjects his family to is cut short when his wife quite literally gets up and walks out of the room, with a rather patronising 'yes, of course, dear'. She is joined by Sheila and summons Eric, leaving only poor Gerald subject to Birling's ongoing monologue. At this point Birling's vulnerability is fully exposed. As has been discussed in the opening analysis, the class divide and Birling's sensitivity to it have been heavily alluded to. Now Birling openly admits to Gerald he is aware of his mother's concerns, and informs him there is 'a very good chance of a knighthood - so long as we behave ourselves'. Stage directions indicate that they both laugh 'complacently' at the prospect of a scandal, clearly viewing themselves and their actions as beyond reproach. This is another sign of arrogance, but also a hint at corruption at the core of the honours list selection process.

As if Birling is not already an unlikeable enough fellow, next he drops in some casually sexist remarks to Eric when he returns, condescendingly advising him that 'clothes mean something quite different to a woman'. Clearly he has not noticed his prospective son-in-law has a particular concern for his appearance - *'rather too manly to be a dandy'*. The use of the word 'dandy' in the stage directions ensures that a director makes Gerald look stylish and fashionable to reflect his *'man-about-town'* persona. This irony that may or may not be lost on the audience. Nevertheless for readers of the play it is another nail in the coffin of Birling's unlikeability.

Birling still hasn't finished, however. Soon he has embarked on another lengthy lecture, ostensibly for the benefit of the young men in his company. Comparing socialism to being 'all mixed up like bees in a hive', he suggests that people caring for our each other is akin to behaving like subhuman insects. At the point he infamously announces 'a man has to mind his own business and look after himself and his own - and -'. Then the doorbell rings *'sharp[ly]'*, and significantly Birling *'stops to listen'*. The significance of the doorbell is discussed elsewhere in this guide, but it is important to point out here that the impact of the Inspector is felt even before he has entered the room. Any interpretation which suggests his supernatural qualities would be supported by Priestley's decision for him to announce his presence at *precisely* this moment. The audience - and wider society - has heard enough of these capitalist arguments, and the interruption brings relief.

Birling's attitude to the Inspector is not unwelcoming, initially. He offers the Inspector a drink in the manner of someone who is used to having the police on their side; one who doles out the judgements as opposed to being on the receiving end of them. He quickly becomes irascibly impatient, however, as it becomes clear that the inspector is not going to behave in the deferential manner Birling expects. Birling grows 'increasingly impatient' as the Inspector describes the death of a young girl. Clearly Birling is unmoved by the incident and ready to take control of the conversation before the inspector cuts him off 'massively', in a manner the audience is likely to find quite enjoyable. The disregard Birling has for the young girl is further reinforced when he struggles to remember her, which is difficult to believe once the impact he has had on her life is revealed. He readily admits he 'discharged her', but clearly sees this as a mundane occurrence of little consequence as it happened almost two years before. It takes the Inspector to point out that Birling's actions could ultimately have resulted in tragedy for her, setting in motion a 'chain of events' which determined her fortune. Again, Birling responds dismissively, introducing the theme which is a key recurrent one throughout the play: 'I can't accept any responsibility'. This back and forth opens the central debate Birling and the Inspector dramatise for the remainder of the play. Many of Birling's points may well have been made by members of the audience in their own homes - but coming from such a discredited source the views feel tainted. No doubt the playwright would hope the interchange might prompt the audience to reflect critically on their own ideas, behaviour and assumptions.

A character who will not change and learns nothing during the course of the narrative, throughout the remainder of the play Birling continues to dogmatically stick to the self-centred principles he holds so dear and was so keen to impart on the next generation. That generation, however, act as foils to his callous dogma, with Sheila and Eric strongly susceptible to the Inspector's cold, hard logic, passionate rhetoric and moral compassion. The end of the play freezes on Birling's 'last laugh'.

Almost hysterically he is pointing at Sheila and Eric, referring to them as 'the famous younger generation who know it all. And they can't even take a joke'. Once again he is interrupted with a bell which rings once again 'sharply'. This time it is the telephone. The curtain falls 'slowly' on the mis-en-scene as he 'looks in a panic-stricken fashion at the others'. One word is used to describe the expression on each of their shocked faces. However much Mr. and Mrs. Birling have tried to squirm and wriggle off the hook of moral responsibility during the play, like a judge passing sentence at the end of a court case, Priestley passes the final, absolute judgement; guilty.

Mrs. Birling

Is there anything good that can be said about Mrs. Birling? Ostensibly, Priestley makes her such a thoroughly dislikeable, uncaring and unsympathetic character that it's impossible for readers or audiences to feel anything but antipathy towards her. Whereas her children learn something profound over the course of the play and change as a result, Mrs. Birling is an entirely static character – she's as heartless, arrogant, selfish and riddled with snobbery at the end of the play as she was at the start. And, indeed, as an imposing, formidable, wealthy matriarch, Mrs. Birling demands respect from others that she doesn't deserve, uses her social capital to try to bully other characters, remains in denial about her son's problems, infantilises him and her daughter, and treats Eva Smith with appalling condescension and callousness. Moreover, she refuses to bear any blame for Eva's tragic death. And on top of that she feels no pity for Eva even after her death, nor any remorse for her own cruel actions.

If it is not possible to sympathise with Mrs. Birling or like her as a character, does Priestley allow us at least to understand why she acts in the way she does? Perhaps. Consider, for instance, her interactions with Inspector Goole. Mrs. Birling leaves the dining-room in Act one before the Inspector arrives and only re-enters the room in Act two, after Mr. Birling and Sheila have revealed their roles in Eva's life and Gerald has also given away his own involvement. So, Mrs. Birling hasn't witnessed the Inspector's questioning of her family. The stage directions tell us that at this point, Mrs. Birling 'enters, briskly and self-confidently'. From her point of view, the evening's celebrations of her only daughter's engagement are in danger of being ruined and she is stepping into the situation in order to sort things out as quickly as possible. If she puffs herself up a little in order to make a strong impression on the Inspector then that is quite understandable. As the stage directions make clear, initially, she is courteous too: 'smiling, social'.

To Mrs. Birling, Sheila's behaviour in this scene is both unexpected and unwelcome. It is socially embarrassing to have her daughter criticise her and to do so so directly and also in front of a stranger. Rather than react with anger, Mrs. Birling observes coolly and perceptively that the Inspector seems to 'have made a great impression' on her daughter. Her instinct is to protect her daughter, giving her an excuse to leave the room, 'you're looking tired, dear'. Perhaps this is overprotective, but it's an understandable maternal reaction. Throughout the scene, Sheila continues to behave erratically, emotionally and out-of-character. Openly contradicting her mother, telling her how she should conduct herself, she makes an obscure comment about not building up a 'kind of wall between us and that girl'. From Mrs. Birling's perspective, this makes less than no sense. As an upper-middle class woman running an upper-middle class household, it is her duty to separate her world from, and raise it above that of the common people. Their class is an essential part of the Birlings' sense of their place in the world and of who they are, and Mrs. Birling does her best to protect this.

To add to the insults, the Inspector also flatly contradicts Mrs. Birling, twice in short succession. Rather than get angry, Mrs. Birling observes mildly that the Inspector's comments are a 'trifle impertinent'. In response Shelia 'gives a short hysterical laugh'. Laughed at, contradicted, embarrassed, badgered, and all in her own home, Mrs. Birling gathers herself rather impressively to protect her family and tackle the Inspector. Sheila, however, seems determined to wash the family's dirty laundry in public, revealing to the Inspector that Eric's 'been steadily drinking too much'. Turning to Gerald for support, Mrs. Birling is then let down by her future son-in-law and has to accept the bitter reality that her own son is becoming an alcoholic, something no mother would wish to hear. Nevertheless, she is composed enough to say to the Inspector that she would be 'glad to answer any questions' he may have.

As attention in the scene shifts to Gerald's affair, Mrs. Birling takes a back seat in the conversation. Her occasional interjections, such as 'women of the town?' and 'Well, really! Alderman Meggarty!', express her understandable distaste at the sordid revelations. Mrs. Birling finds details of Gerald's affair 'disgusting' because she holds herself and her family to a higher ethical code than this. She is right, isn't she; it is disgusting that Gerald used his charm, status and money to play prince charming and sexually exploit a vulnerable young woman.

After Gerald goes out, the spotlight of the investigation swings back onto Mrs. Birling's role in Eva's tragic death. Presented as a wealthy woman, with no need to work, Mrs. Birling could spend her leisure hours in whatever way she saw fit. Surely it is, therefore, highly commendable, and to her great credit, that she used her time productively to help others less fortunate than herself, taking a prominent role in a charity dedicated to the relief of 'women in distress'. Mrs. Birling freely admits that Eva Smith had recently appealed to her charity and, understandably, she was shocked and appalled when the young woman in question called herself 'Mrs. Birling'. Moreover, it is also understandable that, knowing this to be a lie, from this point onwards the real Mrs. Birling mistrusted what Eva had to say.

Furthermore, under the pressure of questioning the young woman had admitted her lie as well as a host of other lies on the back of this, admitting 'that she wasn't married, and that the story she told at first – about a husband who'd deserted her – was quite false'. Only through more questions does Eva concede that she 'knew who the father was'. Surely Mrs. Birling is right to insist that men must not be allowed to impregnate women and then abandon all responsibility for them and for their baby. In insisting on this, isn't she standing up for women's rights and for strong moral values, looking out for the wellbeing of the putative child and holding men to account for their actions? The only reason Mrs. Birling doesn't believe the rest of Eva's story – about her not accepting money and not forcing the young man into a marriage of convenience – is because she had started off with so many palpable falsehoods.

Clearly no charity hands out money willy-nilly. It is incumbent on any charity committee to make careful, painstaking decisions about which projects and which people deserve their limited funds. Mrs. Birling's committee may have helped many other women. How do we know whether her committee didn't refuse Eva help, but still helped other desperate women, women who hadn't lied about their names and their marital status? And she does feel, in fact, some sorrow at Eva's death, 'I'm sorry she should have come to such a horrible end'.

Agree? Disagree? Why? What arguments would you cite against ours? Firstly, you may have noticed that our treatment of this section of the play has been, at best, rather selective and partial. Secondly some of the arguments we used to suggest Mrs. Birling's behaviour was, from her point of view, at least, moral or correct, can also be flipped and seen far less favourably from a different, more objective perspective. Thirdly, even if we accepted the above reading of her character, Mrs. Birling's behaviour from this point onwards in the play is much harder, perhaps even impossible to excuse.

In terms of partiality and selectivity of evidence, we neglected to mention, for instance, the rather important fact that when she is shown the photograph of Eva Smith, initially Mrs. Birling blatantly lies to the Inspector. In addition, other comments she makes belittle Eva's suffering, presenting it as a distasteful inconvenience to the Birlings.

She tells Sheila, for instance, 'to go bed – and forget about this absurd business'. Add to that the way she refuses to listen to her daughter, even though Sheila is quite right, how she attributes Sheila's motivation to 'morbid curiousity' when it is, in fact, unlike her own motivation, driven by a desire to know the truth, how she 'others' Eva, presenting her as inferior, separate and alien - 'I don't suppose for a moment that we can understand... Girls of that class' – and how she tries to intimidate and unduly influence the Inspector with her husband's social standing - 'You know of course that my husband was Lord Mayor only two years ago'.

Examine her behaviour at the charity committee more closely, as the Inspector does, and it's hard to maintain the argument that Mrs. Birling carried out her duties fairly or kindly. Granted, Eva Smith lied about her name and her marital status. However, this was understandable, considering the severe social stigma of being an unmarried mother in Edwardian society, a stigma that might have labelled her automatically as 'undeserving' of help. In any case, her desperate situation as a poor, unmarried pregnant young woman without any means of sustaining herself or any support was readily apparent. As the Inspector powerfully expresses it: 'She was here alone, friendless, almost penniless, desperate. She needed not only money, but advice, sympathy, friendliness...' What did Mrs. Birling when presented with such abject desperation? She 'slammed the door in her face'. If an audience hadn't already arrived at the right conclusion about Mrs. Birling's behaviour, Priestley gives them a shove in the right direction by having Shelia say, 'I think it was cruel and vile'. Moreover, it becomes clear that it wasn't just Eva's lies that lead to Mrs. Birling disbelieving her; Mrs. Birling bigotry prevented her from getting even close to believing Eva.

Mrs. Birling dismisses Eva's explanation that she couldn't accept money from the man who'd impregnated her: 'She was giving herself ridiculous airs,' says Mrs. Birling, 'claiming elaborate fine feelings and scruples… as if a girl of that sort would ever refuse money!' Mrs. Birling is presented as a bigot; she believes working-class people are essentially less moral than their middle-class masters and she is part of a social structure that enforces this prejudice. However, the play reverses the equation; the middle-class characters, and most particularly Mrs. Birling, behave immorally and the working-class characters, Eva and the Inspector, are revealed to be paragons of virtue.

As the play progresses, Mrs. Birling's apparently stern, haughty morality is revealed to be an empty sham. Quite prepared to climb on her moral high horse to condemn the man who'd impregnated Eva and ensure he is 'dealt with very severely' and 'compelled to confess in public his responsibility, she comes back down to the ground with a thud once she learns the man in question is her own son. Once doubts are raised about the Inspector's identity, Mrs. Birling doesn't seem overly worried about Eric's behaviour or his responsibilities. Like her husband she focuses, instead, on how the whole 'scandal' might be covered up and hidden from the public. And only a little after the Inspector has left their house, she is re-writing history [or more bluntly, lying], retreating back into denial, 'I hold him [the Inspector] quite plainly that I thought I had done no more than my duty', 'I was the only one of you who didn't give in to him'. Once again, Priestley uses Sheila to express moral indignation at her parents' behaviour:

Sheila: So nothing really happened. So there's nothing to be sorry for, nothing to learn. We can all go on behaving as we did.

Mrs. B.   Well, why shouldn't we?

Mrs. Birling learns absolutely nothing. She is the 'cold', hard-hearted equal to her husband, but even worse than him, because she was given the last chance to save Eva Smith from a terrible fate. Through her, Priestley suggests that lack of empathy and compassion is not a male-only trait and implies that people of the elder Birlings' generation were beyond reach, unlike their children. Unlike their elders, such children, middle-aged themselves by the time the play was written, could be persuaded of the moral imperative to build a fairer, less prejudiced, more responsible and better society.

Eric Birling

Of all the characters, Eric's misdemeanours are marked out as the worst. His is this final revelation, the most affecting reveal, presented with the greatest degree of rhetorical fervour by Priestley. A few immediate questions arise as a result of this: what makes Eric's relationship with Eva the most traumatic, the most damaging? And secondly, what can be determined about Priestley's perception of class relations as a result of this focus on Eric's actions?

It could be argued that the trauma suffered by the Birlings is a result of the threat to class difference that the pregnancy presents. Eric's relationship with Eva, a working-class woman, threatens to bring the separate worlds of the middle and working classes crashing together. Eric's actions expose the artifice of this constructed difference between the classes. Additionally, Eric's restlessness and alcoholism signal his psychological discontentment.

Yet, the Inspector's interrogation permits Eric to proceed through a process of penitence to come to an understanding of the nature and danger of capitalist and class structures. In this manner, Eric's somewhat redemptive arc allows him, much like Sheila, to demonstrate Priestley's optimism that a younger generation will build what he believes will be a better, socialist Britain in the post-war era.

In line with the established form of the play, the third act again opens with a focus upon the door to the dining room and the cloistered space of the Birlings' comfortably middle class, bourgeois life. In, fact the repetition of this motif is made absolutely clear via the following stage direction: 'Exactly as at the end of Act Two. Eric is standing just inside the room and the others are staring at him'. Once more the door functions as a liminal, or in-between, space between the Birling's protected bourgeoise lives and the chaotic outside space of political and economic conflict, a world both managed for the Birlings' benefit and held at a distance from them. Eric's standing in the doorway as Sybil Birling is forced to accept the true nature of her son's behaviour exemplifies my earlier point: his relationship with Eva threatens to breakdown the separation, the border between these two spaces, to bring the middle-class into the same chaotic unstructured space occupied by the working-class. The horror of this prospect is made evident by Mrs. Birling's dialogue that follows:

> Mrs. Birling: (distressed) Eric, I can't believe it. There must be some mistake. You don't know what we've been saying.

Her clipped dialogue, her insistent tone, coupled with the playwright's signposting of her psychological discontentment emphasise the trauma of this final and most profound of revelations. It is at this point above all that the Birlings' collective, ideological blindness is exposed. The curtain is drawn back to reveal the true nature of the system of class relations that protects them. Mrs. Birling is forced to acknowledge the reality of male bourgeoise behaviour and her family's shared humanity with a class of people she despises.

Eric's own confrontation with and acceptance of his guilt marks out a psychological process totally interwoven with one key aspect of his behaviour: drinking. Eric's drinking is the symptom that reveals his discontentment, the restlessness that underpins his character and can be broadly interpreted as symbolising the broader restlessness of a younger generation. After the Inspector notes that Eric will need his drink, Priestley makes clear via a stage direction Eric's expert relationship with alcohol: 'His whole manner of handling the decanter and then the drink shows his familiarity with quick heavy drinking. The others watch him narrowly.' Whereas Eric's relationship with his family and his father exemplifies a dissatisfaction - a non-expert, peripheral kind of engagement - his familiarity with alcohol is expert. His semi-alcoholic behaviour manifests as a result of such dissatisfaction with his bourgeoise middle-class life. This point is emphasised by Mr. Birling's earlier dismissal of Eric; as Eric attempts to challenge his father in the opening act about the possibility of war and the decline of Edwardian capitalism, Birling shuts him down, instructing Eric to 'let me finish' and declaring that Eric 'has a lot to learn yet'. Eric's rejection of his father's ideology is hinted at this early stage and his drinking becomes a central part of that symbolic and oedipal rebellion in addition to functioning as a means of forgetting or repressing the fact that he is perceived by his father as a disappointment, incapable of inheriting what has been built.

That said, Eric's drinking and rebellious behaviour also have a distinctly more insidious aspect. The exploitative behaviour of the male bourgeoisie, characterised by a systematic sexual objectification of disempowered working-class women, is brought into sharp relief through Eric's behaviour. Eric's character works here to reveal the dark heart of bourgeoise masculine identity; his rebellious behaviour seems almost to parody the more measured and carefully secretive actions of Gerald and even that of Joe Meggarty. Eric is in fact able to reflect critically on this behaviour, as if he has been driven by some external force, conditioned as a result of his gender and class to engage in such exploitative behaviour.

> Eric: Yes, I insisted – it seems. I'm not very clear about it, but afterwards she told me she didn't want me to go in but that – well, I was in that state when a chap easily turns nasty – and threatened to make a row. [...] Oh – my God! - how stupid it all is!

Eric's possible rape of Eva/Daisy is concealed beneath a superficial layer of euphemism and panic. Drinking, and the fogginess it creates in his mind, further conceals the reality of his actions. Eric's immersion in a damaging culture of masculinity is particularly evident from his use of colloquial language alongside euphemism, most evident in his declaration that he 'was in a state when a chap easily turns nasty'. Hesitant, fragmentary speech patterns make clearer again the process of introspection Eric is undergoing as he comes to acknowledge the true nature of his actions, despite his failure to present events in clear terms. Both Eric and Gerald's narratives serve to uncover the violence that underpins sexual politics in a society structured around class difference. Eva/Daisy's pursuit of subsistence forces her to indulge the fantasies of these powerful male figures and even prostitute herself as is hinted by Eric's noting that 'she wasn't the usual sort' and 'some woman had helped her' to establish herself. In part it is through this narrative of gender and class-based exploitation that Priestley demonstrates the intersectional nature of these two factors of identity, drawing a parallel between worker and woman.

The following sequence, in which Eric's taking of £50 from his father's office is revealed, further illuminates the relationship between father and son, providing an insight into the development of Eric's damaging and violent masculinity. Priestley creates a clear conflict between the two, possibly implying that Eric's excessive, violent neurosis is a symptom of distance between father and son, an attempt to prove his masculinity and worth through self-destructive behaviour. Upon discovering the truth about the stolen money, Birling asks 'why did you not come to me when you found yourself in this mess?' Birling's disapproval and distaste is barely concealed. Eric replies by noting that Birling is 'not the kind of father a chap can go to when he's in trouble – that's why.' His final hyphenated clause betrays something of his relief, finally able to reveal the failings of his own father. Nonetheless, the ambiguity present in the phrase 'kind of father' makes clear Eric's continued inability to openly and clearly articulate his emotional experience. Eric emerges in part as victim of a masculine discourse that forbids introspection or open emotional dialogue, while necessitating power and self-assertion. This facet of Eric's character, produced by Edwardian patriarchal culture, in part results in the violent abuse and ultimately the death of Eva Smith.

Much like Sheila, Eric is, however, offered hope of redemption by Priestley. His gradual and increasingly honest introspection results in his acceptance of the Inspector's authority. Eric's acceptance of his family's collective guilt reflects Priestley's optimism for a younger generation whose restlessness and dissatisfaction would in part lead to the victory of Clement Attlee's Labour in 1945 and the creation of the welfare state. Once his interrogation is over Eric expresses allegiance with Sheila, creating the generational divide that expresses Priestley's optimism:

> Eric: Whoever that chap was, the fact remains that I did what I did. And mother did what she did. And the rest of you did what you did to her. It's still the same rotten story whether it's been told to a police inspector or to somebody else.

The repetitive sentence structure, and the comprehensive attribution of guilt with each use of the past-tense 'did' reveals Eric's enlightenment. The Inspector has provided him with an intellectual framework, an analytical method with which to critique the structures that surround and produce him. He is liberated in this moment of acceptance. His enraged declaration also makes clear the structural function of class inequality. Whether there was one or more girls is immaterial to Eric because he has come to understand the systemic character of his family's behaviours. He functions in part as audience surrogate, providing the correct reading of the ambiguity that arises around the Inspector's character. Whereas Birling, Sybil, and Gerald cling to an individualist mode of political analysis in which their behaviours cannot be considered part of a cohesive, structure and system of class relations, Eric and Sheila come to understand that they are part of a system and structure that drives the 'millions and millions' of Eva's to destitution and death. As Eric declares, it is the narrative, the 'rotten story' as a whole that is authoritative here, and not the culpability of any given individual.

The opposition between these two interpretations reflects the opposition between Marxist modes of structural analysis and free market capitalist philosophies, as developed by figures such as Adam Smith and Friedrich Hayek. Where the Marxist understands the individual as an actor within economic and cultural superstructures, the capitalist sees the actions of the individual in pursuit of power as justified and without fault. The generational divide that emerges in part through Eric's character here brilliantly articulates this fundamental opposition.

Sheila Birling

How do you persuade an audience to agree with your point of view? One potent way is to flatter them. Generally speaking the majority of Priestley's audience watching the play for the first time in the 1940s would have, in all likelihood, been middle-aged and middle-class. In 1912, when the play is set, these audience members would have been young men and women. To them, the elder Birlings must have represented their parents' generation, a generation who had sent young men into the Great War but who hadn't actually had to do any of the fighting, or indeed dying. In all likelihood, Priestley's original audience would have identified far more with Eric and with Sheila, representatives of a new generation wanting to change society, to make it fairer, kinder and less prejudiced. And, of the members of the Birling family, including Gerald, Sheila learns the most during the play's action, changes the most, and is surely the most likeable and even admirable.

As a character Sheila Birling fits a familiar literary type, the ingénue. An ingénue is a young, innocent, virtuous, virginial and naïve young woman. Wholesome, good-natured and trusting, often in literary texts she becomes the romantic target of a charming bounder or cad. Sweet-tempered, cossetted from the harshness of the real world and naïve, Sheila has the child-like innocence of an ingénue and, like this character type, she lives under the protection of her father.

Indeed, like the majority of Edwardian women, Shelia is defined through her subordinate relationships with more powerful men. Specifically, as a daughter and a wife-to-be, both her sense of self and her role in society is determined by her relationships with her parents, especially the father who will give her away in marriage, and by her future husband, Gerald Croft, who it transpires has some distinctly caddish qualities. In both of these defining relationships, there is a power imbalance, in both cases working against Sheila's best interests. Hence Sheila Birling can be seen to embody the way Edwardian women were trapped and controlled by the stifling gender mores of their times.

Except that, none of the description above is entirely accurate. It's true that Sheila has some of the characteristics of an ingénue and that both her parents and her husband *try* to shape her identity, *try* to control her understanding of the world and *try* to define her social role. But even at the start of the play, Priestley evokes, but then deviates from the literary convention of the ingénue, making Sheila a less sweet, less doe-eyed and altogether more lively character: Her brother tells us that 'she's got a nasty temper'; she teases Gerald in front of her parents; she uses language that shocks her mother; she holds her own in conversation. Moreover, though her parents may seek to protect, control and influence her, Sheila also seems determined to work some things out for herself. Furthermore, as the play's action unfolds, increasingly, these determining forces are shaken off, sometimes forcefully, so that by the end of the play, Sheila emerges as a stronger, more distinctly individual and independent-minded character – a young woman who, the play implies, will be able to make her own decisions for herself. In a nutshell, Sheila's narrative dramatises a conflict between the type of subordinate woman her parents and her husband want her to be and Sheila's increasing resistance to, and rejection of, this role. By using the ingénue character and then deviating from it, Priestley is able to reflect how young Edwardian women were agitating against their traditionally passive, controlled and second-class roles in society. Albeit in a limited way, and within a cosy middle-class domestic sphere, Sheila's character reflects the wider and more profound resistance of the suffragettes, resistance that was radically re-shaping Edwardian society.

The opening scene of the play is, of course, a celebration of Sheila's engagement to Gerald Croft. In the initial exchanges Sheila may come across as a pretty conventional, middle-class young lady of the period - the rather spoilt daughter of a prosperous family, dutifully attentive to her parents, weepily delighted by an expensive engagement ring. Perhaps calling her mother and father 'mummy' and 'daddy' at her age suggest that she is still child-like and not fully grown-up. But, on the other hand, there are hints that she is bit more spirited and outspoken than the norm. For instance, though her mother instructs Sheila that she will just have 'get used' to her husband disappearing to do mysteriously 'important work' from time to time, Sheila bluntly rejects the advice: 'I don't believe I will'. As well as questioning her fiancé, she also rebukes her brother for being 'squiffy' and behaving like an 'ass' and a 'chump'.

As we mention elsewhere in this guide, Sheila's engagement is discussed by her father in terms of commercial benefits. Gerald is 'just the sort of son-in-law' Mr. Birling 'always wanted', not because he is madly and devotedly in love with his daughter or because Gerald is a kind, compassionate man, or because he is a reliable and decent human being. No, Mr. Birling is delighted by Gerald because this marriage will allow 'Birling and Company' and 'Crofts Limited' to work together and generate greater profits - 'lower costs and higher prices'. And, of course, the events of the play will raise pressing questions about Gerald's suitability as a husband. Yet, even after the disclosure of an affair that Mrs. Birling calls 'disgusting', both senior Birlings are still keen for the marriage to go ahead. Though she appears to feel affection for husband-to-be, Sheila is presented as rather like a valuable pawn in a mutually beneficial financial business transaction arranged by her father.

After the arrival of the inspector, Mr. and Mrs. Birling and Gerald repeatedly try to control what Sheila sees and hears, under the guise of protecting her. Repeatedly, however, she resists this control. When she first returns to the dining-room and asks what's going on, her father tells Sheila that it has 'nothing to do' with her and patronisingly instructs her to 'run along', like a small child. Sheila isn't, however, going to be so easily dismissed, asking the inspector, 'What business? What's happening?'. Similarly, when her father tries to remove her from the investigation, telling the Inspector that the two of them 'talk this over quietly in a corner', she openly interrupts and contradicts him – a bold action for a young Edwardian woman. Furthermore, like her brother, Sheila also criticises her father's treatment of Eva Smith, telling him in plain terms that sacking her was a 'mean thing to do'. Later on, Mrs. Birling echoes her husband's attempts, telling Sheila she's 'looking tired', that she 'ought to go to bed' and that, like a small child after a good night's sleep, she will 'feel better in the morning'. Rather than dutifully accepting her parents' authority, as would have been expected of a well-bred Edwardian daughter, once again Sheila's response is forceful and forthright: 'I'm staying here until I know why this girl killed herself'.

After Gerald has given away his involvement with Daisy Renton he tries hard to keep Sheila from learning the sordid details of his affair: 'All right. I knew her. Let's leave it at that'. Gerald even implores his fiancé to withhold potentially crucial information from the criminal investigation, 'for God's sake – don't say anything to the Inspector'. Moreover, he tries again to remove her from the conversation once the Inspector returns at the start of Act two and yet another time a little later, 'why on earth don't you leave us to it?' And once again, Sheila utterly rejects by her husband-to-be's supposed authority over her; 'nothing would induce' her to leave. Indeed, at times during the Inspector's questioning of Gerald, Sheila takes on the role of interrogator, prompting her fiancé's story, 'Go on… You went down in the bar…' Hardly the behavior of a dutiful Edwardian fiancé or of a gullible ingénue.

The Inspector's treatment of Sheila contrasts sharply with how these other characters treat her. Partly this is because of the way she responds to news of Eva's death. Unlike her father, she is 'distressed' and immediately expresses horror and sympathy. Though the story she tells of getting Eva Smith sacked out of jealous spite hardly reflects well on Sheila, she is consistently regretful and immediately accepts responsibility, unlike her father. In response, the Inspector doesn't try to coddle Sheila or protect her from the truth. Stage directions tell us that he speaks 'harshly' and 'sternly', even when she is expressing remorse. But this harshness doesn't compare with the anger he expresses toward Sheila's parents. And he also treats her with respect, concluding that she really does feel responsible and backing her up when she argues with her domineering mother. Whereas both her mother and father try to maintain Sheila's ignorance of the world - 'It would be much better if Sheila didn't listen to this story at all'; 'I protest against the way in which my daughter… is being dragged into this…' – the Inspector argues that she has a right to know what really goes on: '[*sharply*] Your daughter isn't living on the moon. She's here in Brumley too'.

Of all the characters, Sheila shows the most understanding of the Inspector's message, feels the most sympathy for Eva and expresses the strongest desire to better understand herself and her world. As she tells, her father, girls like Eva Smith area not just 'cheap labour – they're people'. And, as she tells her mother, 'you mustn't try to build up a kind of wall between us and that girl'. Boldly and frankly she tells her mother that her behaviour in turning down Eva's charity appeal was' vile and cruel'. Her mind is also sharper, working more quickly than her parents. When Mrs. Birling is busily blaming the whole tragic affair on the young man who made Eva pregnant, Sheila reads between the lines and, crying, implores her mother to stop. And, of course, when Gerald pieces things together and works out the Inspector wasn't, in fact, a real Inspector and that a girl hasn't died, and when her parents are braying at her and growing hysterical with relief and acting like they have learnt nothing and done nothing wrong, Sheila is shocked and morally appalled, physically edging towards the door, as if to escape. She takes on the role of moral conscience from the Inspector and passes judgements on her parents' behaviour that resonate with the audience:

'But you're forgetting one thing I still can't forget. Everything we said had happened really had happened. If it didn't end tragically, then that's lucky for us. But it might have done.'

Of all the characters, Sheila Birling has the largest narrative arc. As she herself understands, she ends the play a different, and indeed, better character. But we mustn't get too carried away with reading her as a socialist champion, proto-feminist or domestic version of a suffragette. Compare her, for a moment, to the other young woman who remains off-stage and without a voice throughout the play, Eva Smith. Such a comparison reminds us of how privileged and protected Sheila's life has been. It reminds us too that there are issues of class as well as gender at stake in this play. Eva Smith stood up for her fellow workers, was exploited and victimised by Gerald and Eric and was stigmatised, humiliated and rejected by Mrs. Birling. The Inspector has helped set Sheila on the right path, but the play ends before we ever see her put her more enlightened perspective into action. After all, Shelia may move 'towards' the door in the final scene, but she never actually exits.

Gerald Croft

A womanising cad who uses his wealth and power to exploit the vulnerable Eva and expose the enigmatic Inspector, Gerald Croft is easy to read as a metonym for the callous moral indifference of the Edwardian aristocracy. However he is a much more abstruse character than this. Gerald Croft does not fit neatly into either the younger or the older generation and, in a way that appears puzzling to Priestley's socialist agenda and self-proclaimed 'class prejudice', he is apportioned the least blame by the Inspector who remarks 'at least he had some affection for her [Eva] and made her happy for a time'. So, in such a black and white play, where characters are either cruel capitalists or virtuous workers, how morally grey a character is Mr. Croft?

Fundamental to our understanding of Gerald is his role as a metonym for the aristocracy of the Edwardian age. Gerald's superior, aristocratic roots are clear from the beginning of the play, as Birling is sycophantic towards his future son-in-law and can't cover his disappointment at the conspicuous absence of Lord and Lady Croft. In addition, Gerald has a polished, self-assured manner, a manner that was second nature to the Edwardian ruling class. In sharp contrast to the awkward Eric, Gerald is the 'easy well-bred man about town'. He 'insists' on being 'one of the family' and, in a way similar to the Inspector's 'I don't play golf', is able to refuse Birling's offer of a cigar with a blunt 'can't really enjoy them'. Furthermore, Priestley introduces Gerald in a way that creates distance between him and the audience with his first lines in the play being an obscure reference to 'Governor' Finchley being a good judge of port. Speaking on the radio Priestley once said that he felt sometimes that 'you and I - all of us ordinary people - are on one side of a high fence, and on the other side... are the official and important personages'. Gerald's knowing reference makes it immediately clear that he is on the other side of the 'fence', part of an exclusive club to which the audience do not belong. Even Gerald's name reinforces this fact - a 'croft' is a small piece of enclosed land. Hence his name is symbolic of his membership of the propertied class.

Priestley's life-changing experiences during World War One had bred a deep antipathy in the playwright towards the aristocracy, or the so-called 'officer class'. In his memoir, *Margin Released* [1962] Priestley wrote scathingly:

'The British command specialised in throwing men away for nothing. The tradition of an officer class, defying both imagination and common sense, killed most of my friends as surely as if those cavalry generals had come out of the chateaux with polo mallets and beaten their brains out. Call this class prejudice if you like, so long as you remember ... that I went into that war without any such prejudice, free of any class feeling. No doubt I came out of it with a chip on my shoulder; a big, heavy chip, probably some friend's thigh-bone.'

Priestley's experience of class inequality did not end after the war. During his time as a Cambridge undergraduate, Bradford born Priestley felt out of place among upper class young men who he found shallow and immature. Nor did he get along with professors who wanted to meticulously maintain tradition, commenting that 'Cambridge regarded' him 'as a north country lout of uncertain temper'. In light of this context, it is not too far of a leap then, to view Gerald's characterisation as a reflection of this resentment towards an aloof and arrogant class that, whether consciously or not, were responsible for the systematic exploitation of the working class – an exploitation that is laid bare in Gerald's treatment of Eva Smith.

Arguably, of all of the interrogations, Gerald's narrative is the most questionable: Mr. and Mrs. Birling are either too arrogant or ignorant to lie; Sheila and Eric's confessions appear truthful as they come from a place of remorse; but Gerald's account, notably given in front of Sheila, appears highly unreliable. Even before telling his version of events he is very evasive, firstly asking Sheila to keep his secret - 'for God's sake - don't say anything to the Inspector', then asking the Inspector to 'excuse' Sheila, and finally making a flimsy attempt at denying even knowing Eva at all: 'where did you get the idea that I did know her?' Having clearly established that Gerald does not want to reveal his story, Priestley then reveals the full extent of Gerald's lack of credibility by having him construct a narrative in which he presents himself not as a philandering lecher, but instead as chivalric hero who rescued a damsel in distress. Indeed, during Gerald's account, Sheila even remarks she is engaged to the 'hero' of the 'story' and sarcastically accuses him of being the 'wonderful Fairy Prince'.

Beginning with his dubious admission that he 'happened to look' into the Palace Bar for a 'drink'- a bar that just happened to be 'favourite haunt of women of the town' - from the outset, Gerald's narrative is obscured beneath layers of euphemism, evasion and hypocrisy. The diction here is interesting with the noun 'haunt' serving the double purpose of not only revealing the trauma and loss of personal identity suffered by the prostitutes, but also giving us an insight into a misogynistic male bourgeoisie who, perhaps rather ironically here, viewed women as nothing more than ghostly, incorporeal figures. The narrative continues with Gerald sanctimoniously recounting how he rescued Eva from 'notorious rogue' Alderman Joe Meggarty. The audience surely cannot fail to see the arrogance and hypocrisy of a man who believes that what Eva needed that night was to be paid for by the right type of man.

Again, it is Gerald's diction here that reveals the misogyny beneath his pretense of chivalry: When he remarks that 'the girl saw me looking at her and then gave me a look that was nothing less than a cry for help' Gerald's condescending tone and use of the epithet 'the girl' demonstrates his assumed intellectual and masculine superiority over Eva. Indeed, the fact that he even presents his relationship in such a typical, chivalric way actually re-enforces a narrative that women are helpless and given life only by men. But it is perhaps Gerald's description of the end of the affair – 'she was - very gallant - about it' - that is most implausible. Not only does this sound unlikely of a woman whose emotional turmoil will later lead her to take her own life, but the adjective 'gallant' is perhaps being used ironically in a way that serves to remind us that Gerald never was the 'gallant' hero that he portrays himself to be.

There is, however, another way to read Gerald's apparent attempt to portray himself as the 'Fairy Prince'. Perhaps it is more disturbing to imagine that rather than Gerald consciously positioning himself in the role of 'Fairy Prince', he is actually doing it unconsciously. Gerald, like all of the Birlings, bar Eric, begins the play in ignorance of his mistreatment of Eva Smith. Of course, he knows he has had an affair, but he does not recognise that his behaviour towards Eva was in any way pernicious. It is this ignorance that reveals the insidious nature of what Priestley is perhaps most critical of in the play, i.e. the social conditioning that causes people to engage in exploitative behaviour. Just like Birling's capitalist greed, Sheila's infantilism and Sybil's prejudice, it is Gerald's arrogance, his 'easy' belief in the superiority of his class that contributes to the destruction of Eva Smith.

His slippery and euphemistic account is unpalatable, especially to a modern audience. Perhaps even worse, however, is the clear power imbalance that defines his affair with Eva. Throughout the play Gerald's attitude towards women is typically patriarchal; like the senior Birlings, he believes that women should be 'protected' by and dependent on men. But it is in his relationship with Eva that we see the true damage caused by these oppressive attitudes. What initially attracts Gerald to Eva is the thing that makes her vulnerable in that bar - her youth. Misogynistically he expresses hatred for the 'hard eyed dough faced women' that populate the bar and is drawn instead to Eva because of her 'soft brown hair and big dark eyes'. This imagery creates an impression of a vulnerable child, implying that Gerald did not want a woman 'hardened' to the harsh realities of prostitution, but instead a 'soft' fragile one who will indulge Gerald's masculine and aristocratic desire for power and control, a desire likely to be felt more keenly at a time when such inherited power was becoming threatened. Furthermore, in his description of the affair we see that Gerald's treatment of Eva makes her dangerously dependent upon him: he feeds her, is the only person in her life who is 'interested and friendly' and, when she is turned out of her lodgings, he moves her into a 'set of rooms' that we are to read as a space for wealthy young men to entertain their mistresses. While this is well within the realms of acceptable Edwardian male behaviour, for a modern audience Gerald's conduct is unwittingly exploitative, at best, and at worst nothing short of grooming. Even Gerald admits it was 'inevitable' that Eva became his mistress, implying a lack of choice that is further demonstrated by his admission that Eva was 'intensely grateful'.

When the affair ended Gerald moves Eva out of the rooms, telling the Inspector 'she knew if couldn't last'. Even Eva recognised that as a working-class woman she was doomed to be exploited. Again Priestley uses nomenclature to reinforce this point with the name Daisy being a symbol of innocence and purity that has cruelly been cut down, and **Rent**on signally that no matter what story Gerald may construct she is property that has been paid for.

So why then does the Inspector appear to let Gerald off the hook? One possible answer to this question could be found by looking to Priestley himself. The playwright had many mistresses throughout his three marriages. Perhaps the claim that Gerald 'at least he had some affection for her [Eva] and made her happy for a time' is an unsubtle attempt to present adultery not as a terrible vice, but as a means, albeit only temporarily, of happiness. In this light it is not the affair then that matters, it is the promise of something better than Gerald fails to keep - a representation of the most terrible sin committed by the ruling class - having the power to affect change, but refusing to do so.

And if still we are in any way unsure of what Priestley wants us to think of Gerald, we have only to look at the play's ending. Before he leaves Gerald appears to show some remorse for his actions, admitting he is 'upset'. Even more encouragingly, he also defers to Sheila, asking permission to 'come back - if I may'. Gerald's request to return and use of the modal verb 'may' demonstrates a reduction in power relative to Sheila's empowerment and hints at a new model of more equal and empathetic relationships. But these promises of change are left unfulfilled. Instead Gerald becomes the catalyst for a denouement that reveals the full extent of the selfishness and moral inertia of the Edwardian upper class. In his declaration that 'that man wasn't a police officer' and subsequent efforts to prove that 'there were four or five different girls', Gerald discovers a loophole through which all the Birlings, and he himself, can slip their moral responsibilities. In doing so, he acts like a coward, and reveals a moral corruption at the heart of a class that would do anything to preserve their status, privilege and power. Gerald is acting exactly like the WW1 officer class who dodged front line fighting, and the post WW2 propertied class whom the play-wright believed were avoiding their role in post-war reconstruction.

In *Postscripts* Priestley accused this class of being 'a waste of space' who 'fled the cities to the safety of their country hotels'. Gerald's deafness to the Inspector's message is evinced by his final cavalier comment, 'Everything's all right now Sheila. [*Holds up the ring*] What about this ring?' Gerald's offer of the ring signifies his reversion to the patriarchal structures we hoped he had left behind. But perhaps Gerald's biggest sin is that, in finding a loophole, he prevents the Birlings from finding redemption. In doing this he becomes a representation of the way the aristocracy were seen by Priestley to be holding back progress - dead weight in a post-war society crying out for change.

Inspector Goole

The mystery surrounding the identity of the eponymous Inspector Goole is at the heart of the play's enduring appeal. He is a character who seems to defy interpretation - is he a ghost? A clairvoyant? A time-traveller? A symbolic figure of conscience? The question is left tantalisingly unanswered by Priestley. But in giving the character an omniscient, prophetic nature the playwright certainly imbues him with a preternatural quality that makes us view him less as a person and more as a powerful moral force for progressive change.

The enigmatic Inspector enters the play in act one with stage directions stating that he 'need not be a big man' but he must at once create an 'impression of massiveness, solidity and purposefulness.' Priestley here imbues the Inspector with an authority that comes not from his physical presence, but from the force of his moral stance - it is overwhelmingly 'massive' and 'solid' - and his 'purpose': to shatter the fragile comfort of the Birling's bourgeois lifestyle. The lighting which becomes 'brighter and harder' when the Inspector arrives symbolises the revelatory nature of the Inspector's visit. He has come to 'shine a light' not just on to the Birling family, but also onto the harsh realities of capitalism itself. It is no coincidence that the Inspector's 'ring of the front door bell' interrupts Birling's most overtly capitalist diatribe. If this isn't signal enough that the Inspector's role will be to make a clear socialist point his initial interactions with Birling quickly show his progressive, egalitarian values. When Birling, in a thinly veiled threat, tells the Inspector of his position 'on the bench' and of his close relationship with the Chief Constable the Inspector's curt responses of 'quite so' and 'I don't play golf' show he will have no truck with any attempts to assert authority through privilege, status or connections.

These initial interactions are the beginning of a carefully crafted antithesis between Birling and the Inspector, an antithesis designed to emphasise not only the ideological differences between socialism and capitalism, but also to reveal which political system is the more ethical. If Mr Birling is a metonym for what Priestley believes to be the selfishness of capitalism, the Inspector embodies the moral superiority of socialism. The playwright goes to great lengths in the play's opening to create feelings of abhorrence for the capitalist Birling, so the man who interrupts him will be appreciated by the audience.

The Inspector wears a 'plain darkish suit' in contrast to Birling's expensive evening wear, and his curt, matter-of-fact lines are the very opposite of Birling's verbose, 'portentous' speeches. In what should be a clue that the Inspector is not an impartial police officer, he often takes the opportunity to contradict Birling. For example, responding to Birling's assertions of 'Rubbish! If you don't come down sharply on some of these people, they'd soon be asking for the Earth' he counters with 'They might. But after all it's better to ask for the Earth than to take it'. [For a modern audience such a blunt rebuttal might appear bold, but in Edwardian culture such speaking up against one's 'betters' would have been deeply shocking.] Priestley's clear juxtaposition of Birling's and Goole's modes of speech - one puffed-up and self-important and the other measured and analytical characterises the ideological conflict between capitalism and socialism that their argument represents.

The Inspector, though, is much more than simply a foil to Mr Birling. By interrogating the Birlings' personal morality he aims to irrevocably change the family and create a revolution that mirrors the radical socialist movement of Clement Atlee that was poised to take power in 1945. Indeed with both Sheila and Eric the Inspector succeeds. Systematically and 'solidly', he dismantles the facade of respectability behind which each of the Birlings hide their morally questionable behaviour and is relentless in his mission to make each one take personal responsibility. Having a 'disconcerting habit of looking hard at the person he addresses before actually speaking' perhaps asserts his authority, but perhaps also alerts the person in question to the gravity of his purpose. When speaking of Eva, the Inspector makes constant use of emotive language in an ironically matter-of-fact tone - 'burnt her inside out, of course - in order to expose the detachment of the Birlings and those like them. He does this repeatedly and always at moments when the family are resisting his message; he will force them to face what they have done, however much they resist. Arguably this is why the Inspector insists on 'one person and one line of inquiry at a time.'

He says he wants to avoid a muddle'- the 'muddle' being that any sort of group questioning would allow Gerald and the Birlings to escape from the introspection required to truly take personal responsibility.

But it is not just the Birlings with whom the Inspector relentlessly pursues his socialist message, it is with the audience too. The Inspector's visit culminates in a final speech, an exact antithesis of Birling's speech in Act 1, where Priestley makes clear his function as an instructive moral force, not just for the Birlings, but also for those watching from the comfortable theatre seats:

'We don't live alone. We are members of one body. We are responsible for each other. And I tell you that the time will soon come when if men will not learn that lesson, then they will be taught it in fire and blood and anguish. We don't live alone. Good night.'

The grammatical and declarative clarity of the Inspector's claims here raises the authority of his voice above the other characters. Priestley transforms him into a prophetic, absolute moral authority and source of truth, reflecting the playwright's belief in the ethical superiority of socialism. Furthermore, the use of biblical language and a righteous, moral tone elevates him into an almost Christ-like figure. Priestley could be drawing a connection here between socialism and Christian notions of morality. Although there is clear dramatic irony, the use of rhetoric draws a clear parallel between the didactic events of the Birlings' dining room and the theatre itself - a space for the instruction of the post-war audience.

And it is in this instructive function that we see the Inspector as a sort of avatar for Priestley himself. In 1941, the Conservative Minister of Information, Duff Cooper, brought an end to Priestley's popular radio show *Postscripts*. While some historians argue that this was due to contemporary debate around the role of powerful personalities in wartime broadcasting, Priestley maintained that it was due to his show's emphasis on promoting socialist values. This lends credence to the interpretation of the Inspector as Priestley's mouthpiece - he is the voice of Priestley, ungagged and amplified, the dramatic form freeing the playwright to deliver his ideas with renewed vigour and potency. In 1940 Priestley argued that 'We cannot go forward and build up this new world order, and this is our war aim, unless we begin to think differently one must stop thinking in terms of property and power and begin thinking in terms of community and creation' - a line that could have been spoken by the Inspector himself.

However, in the play's final dramatic twist, something Priestley called 'the key to the play' we learn a second Inspector is on his way, thus shattering any ideas about who Inspector Goole is or what he may represent. We may turn to the Russian philosopher Ouspensky - a thinker who had a great influence on Priestley - to make sense of this twist. As we outlined previously, Ouspensky expounded a theory of time as a circle, or indeed a spiral in which those of higher intelligence could ascend to a higher dimension. Perhaps this suggests that Inspector Goole represents what Ouspensky called a 'chosen person'. The upward spiral theory meant that, while moving upwards, an individual - or 'chosen person'- may be able to look down on those lower and help them to avoid making the mistakes that are keeping them forever trapped in their cycle. Inspector Goole would not be the first of these 'chosen people' to appear in Priestley's work, another notable example being Dr Gortler in the aptly named *I Have Been Here Before*. This interpretation casts the Inspector in a rather benevolent light, as someone who has generously taken the time to help the Birling's negotiate their way out of the time-loop and up the spiral. The Inspector offers the Birling's a second chance - something which many of us would covet.

And if this all seems rather fanciful, perhaps this is exactly what Priestley intended us to think. Perhaps he leaves us with an incomprehensible enigma because this is what he intended the Inspector to be; an impossible fantasy. With the genuine Inspector on his way the curtain falls, leaving the audience to predict the happenings and consequences of this repeat interrogation. And what do we think will happen? The very fact that the Police Department phoned in advance to warn Birling suggests that Colonel Robert's friendly influence may be operating cosily and that any wrongdoing by the family might be hushed up. This then makes Inspector Goole and his righteous interrogation an idealistic fantasy of what should happen when powerful and privileged people violate moral codes. While everyone, including the privileged elite, should be forced to take responsibility, to face consequences and to 'never forget' their actions, in practice this hasn't and still doesn't always happen. The jaded Priestley knew this is the way of the world, and so perhaps the Inspector is a dream shared with the audience - his fantasy of a just, egalitarian future. And reading the Inspector in this way, as a fantasy, reveals another important point: a fantasy has the power to affect real change, just consider the characters of Sheila and Eric.

Whichever way we interpret the Inspector, it is certainly true that his social commentary is made all the more powerful by the mystery, and perhaps if we, like the older Birlings, obsess too much about who the Inspector is, we too are in danger of missing the point: Regardless of the identity of the messenger, the time of judgement has come and we all must take a good long, hard look in the mirror.

Eva Smith

Arguably Priestley's characterisation of Eva Smith is the most theoretically interesting in the play. The playwright's decision to make her an off-stage character, removed from the space of the generic parlour room investigation, means that her identity is constructed only through language used by others. As a result, Priestley is able to exemplify the process by which his various bourgeoise characters other and objectify Eva Smith.

She is utilised either as a cipher in the construction of Gerald and the Birlings' own fantasies or her image serves as a demeaned representation of the working-class. Thus, the void Priestley creates via the absence of Eva's own body and voice serves to reveal how both the working-class and women were systematically othered and objectified by the coercive bourgeoise and capitalist Edwardian class system. Alongside this example of systematic objectification, Priestley uses the Inspector's revelation of Eva's suicide as a means of demonstrating the material violence enacted against the working class under capitalism. This characterisation of Eva demonstrates a typically materialist and Marxist analysis of class relations: Priestley demonstrates the material suffering of the working-class as disguised or concealed by the construction of ideology or 'false consciousness'. Both the audience's and the Birlings' realisation of the material exploitation of the working-class comes as a result of a forced and traumatic breakdown of their ideological perception of women and the working-class as other, economic resource and as sexual object.

A crucial aspect of Eva's characterisation, fundamental to a clear understanding of the function of her character, is her role as metonym for the working-class and for working-class women within Priestley's social diorama of Edwardian England. In line with the conventions of the parlour-room murder mystery genre that Priestley draws upon, each character serves to personify, or metonymically represent a stratum of the social hierarchy: Gerald models the aristocracy while Mr Birling the nouveau riche. In line with this, the typical setting of the parlour room within the broader space of the typical Edwardian middle-class house models the class relations that make-up the system of Edwardian capitalism. For example, the parlour room serves as the prime space for performance of middle-class social roles. What place then does Eva have in this society? Most notably, her absence demonstrates that the working-class had no power to influence the construction of this hierarchy; Eva's role is determined by the Birlings who build and maintain the structures of power that they inhabit.

Furthermore, the commonality of the name 'Smith' exemplifies her working-classness, as well as her universality - her metonymic function for the working-class collectively. Her forename Eva further emphasises her universality and function, alluding, albeit in disguised

123

fashion, to Genesis. A range of possible interpretations arise at this point: On the one hand, the name could emphasise her role as an everywoman figure; on the other, Priestley could be ironically signposting Eve's causal role in the fall from grace as, in Priestley's narrative, it is the capitalist class and not a woman that is the source of original sin. Nonetheless, what Priestley makes clear is the universal and metonymic function of the character; Eva embodies both the working-class and working-class women.

Eva is largely defined by her absence, or voicelessness. Her single act of authoritative expression comes in the form of her death. Eva's suicide, her act of self-destruction, it could be argued, exemplifies the alienation, the loss and dislocation of identity that the working-class experienced in Edwardian society. An examination of the way the Inspector describes Eva's suicide helps to elucidate this analysis: 'Inspector: Yes, she was in great agony. They did everything they could for her at the infirmary, but she died. Suicide, of course.' The use of evocative language associated with physical trauma also represents something of Eva's psychological experience and suffering; her shapeshifting, altering of her identity and name in service of pleasing her social superiors' results is a traumatic loss of personal identity.

Her self-imposed agony mirrors the destruction of the self that her social and economic position necessitates. Furthermore, the Inspector's matter-of-fact tone, generated through the adverbial 'of course' defuses the intense pathos usually invoked by the concept of suicide. Suicide is here not a product of unique, individual suffering - some freak incident and tragedy - but rather an inevitable product of the structures of

Edwardian capitalism. The Inspector's cool, analytical mode makes clear the normality of working-class alienation, represented here through Eva's suicide. For Priestley's contemporary post-war audience, as for the Birlings, the structural and inevitable destruction of working-class lives is revealed, no longer excusable as freak, individual tragedy.

Priestley's awareness of Marxist and materialist philosophy is also made clear with the imagery of Eva's death. At the heart of Marx's analysis of economic structures is his distinction between the 'economic base' and 'the superstructure'. The 'economic base' referred to the system of resource production which exploited the worker for their labour, providing them with enough only to survive to most effectively produce profit. 'The superstructure' was the system of culture and language that created ideology and allowed capitalists to justify their actions and their workers to tolerate them. Marx argued that the propaganda and culture that made up the superstructure served to justify capitalism and exploitation. Clearly Mr Birling, with his absolute faith in the progress generated by the market, is immersed in a pro-capitalist ideology or what Marxists call 'false consciousness'.

Eva's suicide and the material description of her death uncovers the operation of the 'economic base', the material exploitation of the worker that occurs under capitalism. Again, the Inspector utilises language that may reduce pathos in his description of Eva's body: 'burnt her inside out, of course'. The same qualifying phrase prevents our perception of the death as a freak tragedy, forcing the critical eye of reader and audience. In addition, the imagery of contortion - 'inside out' - exemplifies the material violence and suffering generated by capitalism. It is also notable that the beauty of Eva's body is spoilt or corrupted. Eva's body and final act of expression remains distant, experienced by the Birlings only second hand. The conscious space of the parlour room is only momentarily and partially threatened by the repressed reality of their collective behaviour. The visceral, but distant, character of the death allows Priestley to sustain a gradual process of traumatic acceptance for the Birlings as opposed to a sudden and forced reveal.

In the opening to this essay, we outlined two broad perspectives through which the audience accesses Eva's character. That of the Inspector we have already attended to; the other was that of the Birlings, each one of them perceiving and constructing Eva as a different constituent object in their own personal realities. If the Inspector's representation of Eva gives her momentary power, revealing her trauma and material exploitation, then the Birlings' visions of her character demonstrate their coercive use of her as a fantasised other in service of their own egos. Birling himself provides our first account of Eva's character, reflecting on Eva's leading the demand for higher wages within the factory: 'if you don't come down sharply on some of these people they'd soon be asking for the earth'. Through his dismissive and demeaning language Birling characterises Eva as disruptive force, as a threat to the authority and power of capital which he worships as a source of progress and power. He constructs a moral system for himself that justifies his 'coming down sharply' upon workers and his systematic exploitation of them. His interpretation of Eva reinforces his pre-existent ideology.

Somewhat contrastingly, Sheila's expulsion of Eva from Milwards does not 'objectify' Eva per se, rather it is a rejection of her as threat to Sheila's own ego. Her overwhelming jealousy must be calmed, resulting in Eva's firing. Both Eric and Gerald, more obviously demonstrate fantasised objectificationa of Eva, rejecting any reality of her experience and instead using her as a means to sustain their own sexual and egoistic fantasies. Gerald provides a clear example of this when describing his first interactions with Eva. Here he notes that 'the girl saw me looking at her and gave me a glance that was nothing less than a cry for help'. His infantilising of Eva and positioning of himself as the 'fairy prince' [as Sheila later derides him] makes clear his construction of a chivalric fantasy derived from medieval Romance. Gerald uses Eva as a feminine and sexual object to sustain this fantasy, much as Mr. Birling uses her to sustain a particular caricature of the working-class.

Sybil Birling does much the same. Her rejection of Eva from her charity and dismissal of her as a 'girl of that class' reveals her perception of Eva as undignified 'whore'. All the Birlings engage in a coercive manipulation of Eva's character to justify their own actions and appease their consciences. The function of the Inspector and the analysis he brings forth is to uncover the violence and distortion that underpins this manipulation. Eric's arc exemplifies this best. His allusion to his possible rape of Eva and failure to explicitly acknowledge this reveals the hidden violence that characterises the exploitations of workers and women. Eric describes himself as 'in that state when a chap turns nasty', only euphemistically acknowledging the repressed knowledge of his sexual abuse of Eva.

One final point that demonstrates Priestley's surprising prescience in political analysis is the clear parallel drawn between woman and worker. The very deliberate decision to have the workers of Birling's factory all female, when most of the working population both in Edwardian and post-war Britain would have been male, makes clear that the playwright intends us to consider the relationship between class and gender. Ultimately, Eva's exploitation for profit as worker is presented in parallel with her exploitation as woman and sex object. In both cases, Priestley illustrates the objectification, and the alienation of the Other. Both as woman and worker, Eva is forced to shapeshift, to adopt a variety of symbolic identities, to perform a variety of roles in order to fulfil the desires of the bourgeoise class. In her changing from Eva Smith to Daisy Renton and in her shifting from seamstress to prostitute, she exemplifies the suffering and destruction of personal identity that comes alongside the disempowerment and the exploitation of individuals. Of course, as the Inspector might add, this could only result in a final, inevitable act of self-expression, a final turning 'inside out' of oneself, a baring of one's psychological and physical torment to an ideologically and cruelly blinkered society.

Edna & other secondary characters

Edna

The Birlings' parlour maid, whose name bears a striking resemblance to Eva, is another representation of an oppressed working-class woman. Like Eva, Edna lacks agency and has no story or real voice of her own. She says and does so little, in fact, that we are almost tempted to overlook her as a character, a mere status symbol of a wealthy family. But on closer inspection, Edna's marginalised and menial role reveals much about Priestley's views on class division.

Indeed, the play opens with a reference to the parlour maid, with Birling asking 'Giving us the port Edna?' This line not only establishes the class divide, but it is the first of many unchallenged commands given to Edna. There are no niceties when the Birling's address her; she is only given orders and, noticeably, never any thanks. Birling speaks to Edna in short imperative sentences best exemplified when she announces the arrival of the Inspector; Birling directs her to 'Show him in here. Give us some more light'. Of course, this treatment of a servant would be nothing unusual in an Edwardian household, but her absolute assent and silence during the interrogations [we could speculate as to what Edna might have to say, if questioned] hints at a profound vulnerability- the same vulnerability that saw Eva fired from the factory: Edna does not have a voice because, as a disposable working-class woman, she cannot afford to speak.

But Edna does though do something extremely powerful in the play –

she opens the door to Inspector Goole. When the Inspector enters under 'brighter' and 'harder' light, which notably Edna provides, it is not really a police Inspector that so disrupts the Birlings' bourgeois existence, but socialism itself. It is therefore significant that Edna opens the door to him. Priestley's stage directions suggest that the working-classes can have power - the power to usher in socialism. Priestley again uses nomenclature to reinforce this point; the name Edna is derived from the Hebrew word for rejuvenation.

Perhaps also, there is a more subversive element to Edna's role in the play. As previously mentioned, Edna's marginal role can make it all too easy for us to overlook her. This is especially the case when we are reading the play; as Edna has so few lines we can easily forgot she is present in scenes. Even when we can see a physical character in a stage production, performing physical actions, our attention is always being directed elsewhere. Is this another theatrical coup by Priestley? In a play centered on the exploitation of a working-class woman, ignoring Edna seems in some ways perverse, and as such potentially makes readers and audiences complicit in the disregard of working-class women.

Sir George and Lady Croft

Gerald's aristocratic parents are conspicuous by their absence from their son's engagement party. Confidentially Birling reveals to Gerald that he has an 'idea' that Lady Croft feels her son 'might have done better for [himself] socially'. Their absence from the family dinner seems like a social snub and suggests that his fears may be justified.

Nevertheless, Birling has received 'a very nice cable' which demonstrates that they will not object to the marriage, perhaps out of necessity. The Industrial Revolution had meant that the balance of power had shifted from the landowners to the manufacturers as the wealth of entrepreneurs like Birling grew beyond that of their social superiors. This then allowed for marriages of convenience where aristocrats gained wealth and manufacturers gained status. It is not only Gerald and Sheila's marriage which can be perceived in this way, but perhaps Mr. and Mrs. Birlings' too. As the initial stage directions make clear, she is his 'social superior' and Mrs. Birling tries, from time to time, to correct some of her husband's less polished behaviour.

But wealth doesn't seem to be quite enough for Lady Croft and Birling knows this. In a desperate attempt to prove his worth, tells Gerald he has a 'chance of a knighthood'. Gerald's eagerness to tell his mother and his belief that she would be 'delighted' reveals a snobbery that marks the Crofts as the type of establishment aristocrats that Priestley disliked so intently.

Alderman Joe Meggarty

As an elected official, 'horrible old Meggarty' is an example of the ways in which seemingly reputable people can act in disreputable ways. He is a respected member of Brumley high society, yet frequents the Palace Bar in search of prostitutes. Gerald's description of him as 'half-drunk and 'goggle-eyed' is revolting. Gerald also recounts how Meggarty 'wedged [Eva] into a corner with that obscene fat carcass of his'. Gerald's diction is interesting here - 'carcass' is, of course, the body of a dead animal, almost as if he recognises that the type of 'sots' and 'rogues' that Meggarty represents are waste products of society. [Of course Gerald fails to recognise the irony that he too could fit into that unpleasant category.] Again, Priestley's name choice is interesting here: Joe is an everyman name, suggesting Meggarty represents any sleazy official who uses their societal position and status to exploit others.

Mrs. Birling's shocked reaction to Gerald's revelation - 'surely you don't mean Alderman Meggarty' - prompts Sheila to reveal that Meggarty's 'womanising' is something that 'everybody' knows about. Everybody except Mrs Birling, naturally. Her shocked reaction exposes not only the myopia of the Edwardian bourgeoisie, but also their crass hypocrisy. Whereas she dismisses the idea that Eva Smith could have behaved with moral scruples, Mrs. Birling is desperately unwilling to accept that those in positions of wealth and power can behave immorally. This desperation is also shown by Mr. Birling, who 'sharply' cuts Sheila off when she begins to tell of the poor girl who only 'escaped' Meggarty with a 'torn blouse'.

Chief Constable Colonel Roberts

Following the Inspector's particularly zealous socialist assertion of 'it's better to ask for the earth than to take it', Birling asks the Inspector if he knows 'our' Chief Constable Colonel Roberts, an act of name-dropping clearly designed to be intimidating. He 'warns' the Inspector that he and Roberts are 'old friends' who play 'golf' together, making it clear to the audience that there is an exclusive club of the political and social elite in Brumley. Further evidence of the pally relationship between

Birling and the Chief Constable comes at the end of the play when Roberts takes Birling's late night phone call and confirms that there is no Inspector Goole.

An audience must question why Birling and Colonel Roberts are seemingly keen to maintain such a familiar relationship. Certainly the Inspector is not interested in garnering any favour with Birling. The relationship between Birling and Roberts could be seen as a kind of cronyism. Furthermore, it may, indeed, indicate the operation of an oligarchical system, where those with wealth and influence mutually benefit from each other, while others are excluded. This is a system that ultimately perpetuates the sort of inequality that Priestley so wanted to eliminate. In this light, Roberts' lack of a speaking role in the crucial revelation about Inspector Goole has a disturbing aspect: It emphasises the far-reaching, potentially damaging, potentially corrupting, influence of those with power.

Politics, characters and sympathy

The Romantic poet, John Keats coined the term 'negative capability' to describe what he considered to be a key aspect of the genius of great writers. Negative capability, Keats said, is the ability to remain in doubts and uncertainty about something. In the work of William Shakespeare it allows the playwright to occupy opposing viewpoints without, Keats argued, tipping the scale firmly in one direction or another. The same cannot, however, be said to be true about Priestley's play. Whether that is a strength or a weakness we'll leave you to decide.

Clearly Mr. and Mrs. Birling represent one end of the scales in An Inspector Calls and Inspector Goole represents the other. A 'sound useful party man' with a 'very good change of a knighthood', as he himself attests, the middle class, bourgeois Mr. Birling embodies employers and 'the interests of capital'. With his talk of taking responsibility for each other, for society as 'one body' and sympathy for the lives of 'Eva Smiths and John Smiths', contrastingly the Inspector expresses socialist values. And their different political ideologies are weighed on the scales of the play's action. On the one side is a conservative version of capitalism and on the other progressive socialism. On these political scales we can also place Gerald Croft with the elder Birlings and Eva Smith with the Inspector. Whereas the position of these characters is fixed and static, as the play develops the remaining main characters, Sheila and Eric, move significantly from one pole to the other, from closer to their parents' side to closer to the Inspector's.

Priestley tips the balances of the scales in several ways to ensure that conservative capitalism is made to seem far less attractive to the audience than socialism. Firstly, the elder Birlings are presented as fundamentally dislikeable, crass and self-satisfied characters. Secondly, they are shown to get many things wrong, blithely misreading and  misunderstanding the world around them. Thirdly, Priestley makes the audience react sympathetically to Eva Smith's suffering, primarily at the hands of the Birlings, and fourthly he presents the Inspector as the most powerful, perceptive and articulate character in the play.

Dislikeable Birlings

Mr. Birling is self-centred, 'hard-headed' [a phrase that suggests both hard-heartedness and stupidity], pompous and boastful. As a parent, he shows little understanding of, or tenderness towards, his son, and he is happy to use his daughter to further his business interests. As an employer, he treats all his workers badly, coming down hard on Eva Smith when she tries to stick up for herself and her fellow workers: 'If you don't come down sharply on some these people, they'd soon be asking for the earth'. Yet, clearly, Birling makes a very nice living from their labours and the Inspector implies that his behaviour is driven by avarice: 'It's better to ask for the earth than to take it'. When the Inspector first arrived, Birling tried to intimidate him by making some unsubtle comments about his social and political connections, a tactic that his wife will repeat later in the play: 'How do you get on with our Chief Constable, Colonel Roberts?... I ought to warn you that he's an old friend of mine'. Later he also threatens to report the Inspector to his superiors.

Even less attractive and more serious is the way Mr. Birling refuses to take responsibility for his role in Eva Smith's suicide. Showing little emotion and no sympathy for the young woman's death, Mr. Birling says curtly that he 'was quite justified' in his actions in sacking her. At the end of the play, once doubt has been cast over the Inspector's true identity, he seeks to cover-up his family's behaviour, including covering up a crime. Like his wife and unlike his children, he learns nothing from the evening's revelations and will happily revert to his previous behaviour. All of this make him a very unattractive character.

Mrs. Birling, of course, has many similarly dislikeable qualities. Perhaps, indeed, Priestley makes her even worse than her husband: The brutally callous way she dismissed Eva/ Daisy's pleas to her charity committee; the horribly snobbish way she dismissed the possibility that a working-class girl could have behaved ethically ['As if a girl of that sort would ever refuse money']; her complete lack of regret and her refusal to take responsibility. Add to this her pride in her own behaviour, her pig-headedness and her lack of even a scrap of compassion. All these and more could be cited against her.

The Birling family and Gerald are middle class, they have social and financial capital and can exert control other their lives. Up until the evening when the Inspector arrived, they have never been held to account for their selfish and damaging actions, nor have they had to justify their place in a society built on social injustice between the classes.

'Unsinkable, absolutely unsinkable'

One reason Priestley sets the play in 1912 is so that he can use dramatic irony to make Mr. Birling seem to the audience to be an arrogant and complacent fool. Priestley lays on the dramatic irony with a trowel, particularly when we are first introduced to Mr. Birling. Birling, it seems, gets absolutely everything wrong: He dismisses 'silly pessimistic talk' about 'labour trouble' and about the possibility of a war. Whereas, of course, the audience know WWI will break out just two years after the play is set. His confidence that 'we're in for a time of steadily increasing prosperity' is, of course, horribly misplaced. If we haven't already got the message that this man is a dangerous idiot, full of hot air, he is then made to cite the 'Titanic' as conclusive evidence that the world is progressing in  an unstoppably positive direction. Not only that, Birling then predicts that 'in twenty or thirty years' time', i.e. the post-WWII period in which the play's original audience would have lived, everyone will have 'forgotten these Capital versus Labour agitations and all these silly little war scares'. Birling also dismisses the warnings of writers - 'these Bernard Shaws and H.G.Wellses' – writers who, in this regard at least, history proved to be right.

While, in theory, we could detach the political ideology from a character who is meant to embody it, it's hard for us to do so. Logically Mr. Birling could be dislikeable, self-centred, arrogant and foolish, but he could still be right about the best ways to run a society. Similarly, he could have horribly misread what history had in store and yet be right that conservative capitalism is more attractive than socialism. Just because someone is wrong about some things, doesn't mean that are wrong about everything. But clearly, Priestley wants us to discredit the ideology by making such an unattractive character embody it.

Sympathy for Eva

Though we never meet her as an on-stage character, Eva's story encourages the audience to feel pity for her: A poor, working-class girl, she is sacked from Birling's employment for seeking better conditions, dismissed from Milwards through no fault of her own, sexually exploited by both Gerald and Eric, made pregnant and a potentially unmarried mother at a time when this was considered utterly shameful, humiliated by Mrs. Birling and refused charity when she was most direly in need. Driven eventually by despair to suicide, she is a victim of all the Birlings and of a society that trapped, exploited and punished her. In addition, we learn later from Gerald that she was an orphan. On top of this, what we hear of her personal traits make us also feel sympathy and even admiration. Moreover, Eva has a powerful advocate to bring her story to light and make the Birlings and the audience care what happened to a young woman who embodies the struggles of the Edwardian working class.

Although Mr. Birling can see nothing admirable in Eva's behaviour as his employee, Eric and the audience can. Birling describes her as a 'lively good-looking girl', a 'good worker' whose abilities made her a good candidate for promotion. Birling uses the word 'ring-leader' to describe the way Eva stands up both for herself and for her fellow poorly paid workers. While Birling uses this term to condemn Eva, most audiences are likely to admire her behaviour. It would take courage nowadays for a poor and lowly worker to stand up to a wealthy and exploitative employer, like Birling, an employer on whom they depended for their livelihood. How much more so this must have been the case in Edwardian England. A working-class man would be expected to defer to a middle-class man, a worker defer to an employer and a woman defer to a man. In this context, Eva's actions show a truly remarkable amount of courage, on top of which, she stands up not just for herself about also for her fellow workers, so she behaves selflessly. To nudge the audience to come to this conclusion Priestley has Eric say, 'Why shouldn't they try for higher ways? We try for the highest possible prices. And I don't see why she should have been sacked just because she'd a bit more spirit than the others'. Well, quite.

We learn that she behaved bravely and stoically when Gerald broke off his affair with Eva. Mrs. Birling adds to our understanding of Eva's virtues when she snobbishly and scornfully opines that Eva 'was giving herself ridiculous airs' and 'claiming elaborate fine feelings and scruples' despite the desperate situation she was in. Later we learn that Eva had indeed protected Eric, despite the fact that he may have rather forced himself upon her, and that she had indeed refused to accept money from him when she discovered it was stolen.

The Inspector also plays a vital role in ensuring the audience side strongly with Eva. Repeatedly he uses emotive and visceral language to reminds us of the terrible manner of her death: 'This afternoon a young woman drank some disinfectant and died, after several hours of agony'; 'a girl died tonight. A pretty, lively sort of girl, who never did anybody any harm. But she died in misery and agony – hating life'; 'Her position now is that she lies with a burnt-out inside on a slab' and so forth. In his exchanges with Mrs. Birling, the Inspector provides a counternarrative of Eva's life and behaviour to Mrs. Birling's scornful one: 'She was here alone, friendless, almost penniless, desperate. She needed not only money but advice, sympathy, friendliness…and you slammed the door in her face'. The Inspector also keeps a major detail of Eva's death back so that he can reveal it when it can have most emotional impact: 'Then the next time you imagine it, just remember that this girl was going to have a child'. As he used Eric in Act one, here Sheila acts as on-stage audience guiding the off-stage audience's response: 'No! Oh – horrible – horrible!' And, of course, in his powerful closing speech, the Inspector tells the Birlings and the audience explicitly that we have a responsibility to care for the 'millions and millions of Eva Smiths and John Smiths still left with us, with their lives, their hopes and fears, their suffering and chances of happiness, all intertwined with our lives'.

Whereas the Birlings and Gerald have agency and some control over their lives, Eva is a victim, a victim of the Birlings certainly, but also of the overarching values structuring her society and enforcing her constricted place within it. The class system, capitalist ideology and Edwardian attitudes to gender, in particular, are as much to blame as the Birlings for her death.

A perceptive and prescient Inspector

In many ways the classless Inspector is presented as an opposite to Mr. and Mrs. Birling. An admirable, steadfast character, he is clever, determined, compassionate and, despite the class-conscious society in which he exists, entirely undaunted by the powerplay of his social superiors. As we've noted, Priestley uses the play's temporal setting to create dramatic irony at the expense of the senior Birlings, making Mr. Birling, in particular, look like an arrogant fool. In stark contrast, the Inspector is presented as a prophetic figure. With keen-eyed perception, he is able to stare into the seeds of time and see which grains will grow and which will not. In the closing speech we have just quoted, for instance, the Inspector, imagines that if Edwardian society doesn't learn from the play's lesson about social responsibility, then it 'will be taught it in fire and blood and anguish', a clear reference to the two World Wars. If the reliable, superior and priest or even Christ-like Inspector believes in socialism, then, the play suggests, perhaps we should too.

Students' work

Before we encourage you to identify everything that is wrong with the first essay, you might be reassured to know that the essay wasn't in fact written by a student. Rather, it is an amalgam of many essays we've read during years of teaching. So, there's nothing to stop you from ripping it apart! In fact, to encourage you, we'll award five points for each problem you identify. Once you've done this, check your total against ours. Sometimes the problem will be something incorrect; at other times the phrasing, terminology or expression could be better.

1. How far does Priestley present Mrs. Birling as an unlikeable character in *An Inspector Calls?*

Mrs birling is a really horrible old woman married to mr Birling and mother to Eric and sheila. In the book she is really snobbish and 'cold' at the start and then when it's her turn to be interrogated by the Inspector ghoul she tells him how she rejected Eva Smith's charity appeal because she had lied about her name and put on ridiculous airs and graces for a working-class girl saying she wouldn't accept stolen money even though Eva Smith was pregnant with Eric's child, although Sibbel didn't know this to be fair. Then, after these people discover that Inspector Goole wasn't a real Inspector Mrs. Birlings, like her husband, pretend that nothing at all has really happened and she doesn't seem to have learnt anything at all about social responsibility, the main theme of the play. Overall, misses birlings is a very dislikeable, horrible person in The inspector Calls which is a didactic play written in the 1940s but set before WWI.

Probably you suspect we're exaggerating. Maybe so, a little. But many of the problems with the introduction are commonly found in GCSE exam scripts.

1. Get titles right; the name of the play and the names of characters. In this example, Mrs. Birling is incorrectly referred to three times. Mr. Birling and Sheila are also referred to incorrectly and the title of the play is, of course, *An Inspector Calls*. If a student is sloppy about this basic level of accuracy why should the examiner believe that they'll be more careful when dealing with more complex issues of analysis and interpretation? [30 points].

2. The phrasing of the essay question ['how far...'] suggests that there may be ways in which we could sympathise with or find something sympathetic about Mrs. Birling. The question also invites us to form a line of argument. These prompts are ignored by the candidate. [10 pts.]

3. 'In the book' doesn't tell us what sort of a book this is and there are many sorts of books. As lots of students fail to distinguish between novels and plays it's a good idea to establish this distinction straightaway. [5 pts.]

4. There's nothing factually incorrect about the second sentence and the student would be earning a few marks for showing knowledge of the play. But, it's narrative summary, in a rather rushed and breathless style. It would be strengthened if some inferences were drawn from the details. That, for instance, Mrs. Birling's treatment of Eva Smith is high-handed, heartless and cruel. Better still if the candidate lifted their head above

character level to consider the question from the writer's point of view. 'Priestley presents Mrs. Birling as a cold and snobbish character' is better than 'Mrs Birling is a cold and snobbish' 'person' or 'woman'. Why? Because in the former the fact that she is fictional character created by a writer for a purpose is explicit, whereas in the second example Mrs. Birling is treated as if she were a real, living human being. [5 pts.] The same issue is evident in the phrase 'really horrible woman' [5 pts.] The sentence is also too long and would be better broken down into two or three sentences. [5 pts.]

5. Although the information isn't incorrect in the sentence, the inexact phrasing creates ambiguity. Specifically, 'she' is used several times when the pronoun could refer to either Mrs. Birling or Eva Smith. [5 pts.]

6. The compressing of so much narrative into one sentence causes some inadvertent misrepresentation. For instance, it appears from this paragraph that Mrs. Birling knew Eva Smith was pregnant when she refused her charity, when, in fact, Mrs. Birling doesn't discover this information until later in the play and with devastating effect. [5 pts.]

7. The penultimate sentence makes a reasonable point. But it would be much stronger if Mrs. Birling's reaction was contrasted to Sheila and Eric's, and this, in turn, was linked to Priestley's aims in writing the play. [5 pts.]

8. While it is useful to contextualise the play, both in terms of when it was written and when it is set, here this information is tagged onto the end of the paragraph. A stronger response would link the settings to the characterisation of Mr. and Mrs.

Birling and to Priestley's overall aims and purposes. It is also always useful to be precise about dates. [10 pts.]

Total: **85** points

How might this essay develop? Typically, students who start with narrative summary tend to continue in this way and their essays tend to follow the narrative structure of the set text.

At the start of the play Mrs. Birling is described as a 'rather cold woman' and she is from a higher class than her husband. When he compliments their cook, for instance, Mrs. Birling corrects his behaviour. She is excited by the marriage of her daughter to Gerald and is impressed by the expensive ring. After this has been presented to Sheila, Mrs. Birling and her daughter retire to the drawing-room leaving the men to talk.

Mrs. Birling doesn't appear again in the play until Act two after the Inspector arrives. When she comes back in she is feeling confident and challenges the Inspector in a way that is similar to her husband. She doesn't listen to Sheila's warnings and gets very agitated when both her daughter and the Inspector contradict her. She also pretends to know nothing about Eva Smith. Mrs. Birling is shocked and appalled to hear about Gerald's affair with Eva/ Daisy. Later in the play the Inspector's questions expose Mrs. Birling's own role in Eva/ Daisy's death.

Okay, this time we won't go through all the things that could be improved in this essay. We'll restrict ourselves to four major points. Firstly, while the essay does show some decent knowledge of the events in the play there's less evidence of understanding. Generally the candidate describes events, but doesn't draw any inferences about their significance in terms of shaping our perceptions of Mrs. Birling. Secondly, some key ingredients are conspicuously absent: Priestley, reference to stage directions and quotations. Quotes, of course, help candidates to focus on the specific words the writer uses and to consider their effects and significance. Thirdly, there's no line of argument with the 'who far...' aspect of the question ignored or forgotten. Lastly, the discourse markers, such as 'at the start', 'when', 'after' and 'later', are all temporal, indicating the essay follows the chronology of the text. Though this is not necessarily a bad idea, it is often a sign of a limited, narrative-based approach. Ideally the candidate would be developing an argument and would, therefore, use discourse markers such as 'therefore', 'hence', 'moreover', 'however', 'consequently' and so forth.

2. Explore the theme of responsibility in *An Inspector Calls*.

J.B. Priestley wrote 'An Inspector Calls' in 1945 during a significant period historically for England. Emerging from the devastation of two world wars, people were determined to build a better, more caring society, leaving behind a decade blighted by mass unemployment and economic depression.

1912 was a time of huge inequality and rigid gender and class boundaries. This choice of setting allows the audience the benefit of hindsight, allowing us to appreciate how ironic are Mr. Birlings' views. For example, he believes that the Titanic is 'absolutely unsinkable' and 'nobody wants war'. The setting also

encourages a parallel to be drawn between the events of the play and society's
failure to learn from the First World War.

Though the contextual knowledge is impressive and is used to explain dramatic effects, the essay needed to engage sooner with textual details.

Priestley uses 1912's unequal society to demonstrate that a fair society depends on compassion and responsibility for our fellow citizens. The play raises the question of the extent that society is responsible for individuals and their problems, such as Eva Smith. Priestley uses her to represent the innocence of all people, which can be destroyed if they are not given the dignity deserved.

This essay continues to demonstrate a sophisticated understanding of how context influences Priestley's text. This is made directly relevant to the specific question asked. (The essay is focussed, clearly answering the question, and the argument is made more apparent by the end of this paragraph.

> *This is shown as we learn of the destructive and selfish attitudes of the Birlings towards Eva's situation: Mrs Birling, for example, cannot see how the suicide of a lower class person affects her or her family. Snobbishly she dismisses people like Eva, calling them 'girls of that class'. Mrs Birling takes no responsibility herself, forcefully arguing that Eva 'only had herself to blame'. Similarly, Mr Birling, has no compassion for Eva. Like his wife, he maintains that her tragedy was her own fault: 'and then she got herself into trouble?' By portraying Eva as the innocent victim of other people's selfishness and by presenting these other people unsympathetically, Priestley implies*

that the Birlings are wrong and that 'we are responsible for each other'.

This candidate knows the play well and is able to use apposite, embedded quotes to illustrate their point. The response is critical and shows good engagement with the wider significance of character (Mrs Birling in this case). The depth of understanding is displayed in the discourse marker 'similarly' indicating that the point is going to be explained in more depth.

> *Inspector Goole is another tool used by Priestley to express his message. The Inspector could be seen as an instrument of justice in the play, persuading the characters to admit their guilt and accept responsibility. In this sense, he is a vehicle for Priestley's own political conscience. Throughout his interrogations, the Inspector sticks to his principle that 'if you're easy with me, I'm easy with you'. Consequently, he delivers powerful moral judgements on the characters, especially those who refuse to accept their crimes. Birling, for example, declares that 'I can't take any responsibility' to which the Inspector responds with 'Public men have responsibilities as well as privileges'. In a similar way, Mrs Birling will not accept that she is to blame, stating bluntly: 'I've done nothing wrong'. Hence the Inspector's tone is harshest with her in his flat, direct echoing and contradiction of what she has said: 'I think you did something terribly wrong'.*

The candidate continues to show critical awareness of how Priestley uses his characters to make a moral/political point. However this also shows a critical response to the significance of the language with the carefully chosen quotes and the brief discussion of the significance of the language. It also impresses with the fluency and coherence of the writing, using discourse markers (Another way...) to signal the flow of ideas from one to the other.

> *In contrast, a more optimistic hope for the future is signalled by how the younger characters accept their guilt. The younger generation are presented as having the will and desire to build a less selfish society and to learn to take responsibility. In contrast to her parents, Sheila, for example, readily admits her guilt: 'It's was my own fault'. The strongest example of the need for social and moral responsibility comes in Act III in the Inspector's final speech. He speaks of all people as being 'intertwined with our lives' and employs powerful, biblical language to threaten the characters into changing. If they refuse to change they will bring a biblical punishment: 'They will be taught it in fire and blood and anguish'. Taking on the language of prophet, the Inspector is able to persuade the audience of the need of collective responsibility. Through hindsight, we recognise that the Inspector is speaking about the Second World War. The audience may then feel that if they adopt unselfish attitudes, they may prevent another repeat of the war.*

This reveals a good grasp of the effects of the language Priestley uses here. However, more impressive in many ways is the complex grasp of context, acknowledging the chronological difference between the setting of the play and its reception by an audience, indicated by 'through hindsight'.

At the end of the play, when they discover that Goole was not a real inspector, some of the characters believe they can continue as they have always done. Gerald's revelation here was a test of what the characters have learnt. Birling, for example, is shown not to have changed: 'The whole thing's different now'. Throughout the play, Birling has argued that 'a man has to look after himself and his own,' demonstrating his selfishness and heartlessness. Similarly, Mrs Birling is more upset by the Inspector's tone than anything she learnt that evening: 'so rude – and assertive'. In the final scene, however, these characters are taught their lesson, as the Inspector prophesised, when they receive a telephone call to say that 'a Police Inspector is on his way here to ask some questions'. As this scene is a direct repeat of earlier events, Priestley clearly emphasises that there is no escape from the responsibility for our own actions.

This is a perceptive point revealing sensitivity to the significance of the language Mrs Birling uses.

Priestley promotes an ideal of social responsibility throughout the play. Voicing his own conscience through the words of the Inspector and through the play's events as a reflection of society and the two world wars, he portrays the attitudes of the elder characters as selfish and mean-spirited. Priestley also encourages us all to adopt the attitudes of the younger characters, thus similarly advocating directly to the audience the need for a collective sense of society.

Comments:

BAND 9 - This essay achieved **full marks in the English Literature GCSE!**

✓ Fluent and well-focussed style answering the question clearly. Discourse markers represent cohesion and the grammar and spelling is accurate.

✓ A critical awareness of the significance of language is displayed.

✓ Apposite quotes are used throughout the essay revealing a wide-ranging knowledge of all facets of the play.

✓ A secure knowledge of the historical context.

So, now your task is to read our last example and mark it yourself. To make your marking accurate we suggest you use the marking criteria for the specification you're following. Usually this criteria can be found on the board's website and is a source of invaluable information for teachers and pupils.

3. Compare and contrast the presentation of Mr. Birling and the Inspector in the play "An Inspector Calls" by J.B. Priestley.

In the play "An Inspector Calls" by J.B. Priestley, Mr. Birling and the Inspector are characters which contrast quite a lot and possibly even clash. Mr. Birling is an arrogant, self-loving, middle-class man who cares only for himself, his money and his status. The Inspector is the voice of reason and justice, managing to make the Birling family and Gerald Croft admit their mistakes and feel remorse for their part in Eva Smith's death.

Arthur Birling is happy to use his power and influence to bully people into doing what he wants them to do. He only cares about how he appears to people and tries to impress Gerald Croft [his social superior] by buying the same port as his father does. His relationships with other characters within the play seem slightly forced and he fails to understand both Shelia and Eric, his own children. He finds it difficult to relate to other characters and refuses to accept that his opinions or actions may be wrong. For example, "A man has to make his own way-has to look after himself-and his family too, of course, when he has one-and so long as he has that he won't some to much harm". In this quote Birling is lecturing Gerald and Eric about life as a man. He makes a very long speech about it to them, as he feels he has earned the right to do this because he is older. Mr. Birling respects only characters that are of a higher social status than him and looks down on people both younger and lower status than him. Also the phrase "and his family" seems to be ironic, as later on in the play it's revealed he has no idea about all the wrong-doings his family has done.

In contrast to this, the Inspector doesn't use his power to gain what he wants but uses "hard-looks", and often blunt and deliberately harsh language. He doesn't care about whether he comes across rude, as long as he is able to find out what he wants to know. He is able to find out exactly what he wants to know and dominates the room, even though he is the person with the lowest social status present. He treats everyone in the same way and doesn't look down on younger people, like Mr. Birling does. However, he doesn't look up to people of higher status like Mr. Birling does either. The relationships he builds in the play are not friendly loving ones, but merely business relationships which he feels are a necessity for his job. For example, "Don't stammer and yammer at me again, man. I'm losing all patience with you people." This is the part in the play where Inspector Goole loses all patience with Mr. Birling. In

1946, when the play was first performed, the audience would have been shocked at this because it was disgraceful and unheard of for anyone to speak to their social superior in this way. Overall, although the Inspector is sometimes rude, he deals with all the characters well and relates to everyone in the same way. Mr Birling has class status and is class conscious, whereas the Inspector doesn't and isn't.

The language Mr. Birling uses is rather flouncy and boastful. From the very beginning Priestley uses dramatic irony to turn the audience against Birling and we soon realise just how ignorant of the world he really is. Birling often uses language which is selfish and the audience get the impression that he loves the sound of his own voice. For example, "and I say there isn't a chance of war". This extract uses dramatic irony because this play was set before the 1st world war, but written after the second, so the audience know that there has been a war. J.B. Priestley uses dramatic irony, almost too much, to make the audience laugh at Birling's arrogance and stupidity. At the time when the play was written Birling was a typical, slightly over-exaggerated capitalist and we can tell this from the language he uses throughout the play. Capitalism is an economic system characterised by private property ownership, companies competing for their own economic gain and free market forces to determine the prices of goods and services.

In contrast to this, the Inspector is to-the-point and slightly patronising with his language. The Inspector is a socialist; many think he is Priestley's mouthpiece, as he was a socialist himself. Socialism is an economic system which is based on cooperation rather than competition and which utilizes centralised planning and distribution. The Inspector's language is cold and impersonal, but everything he says has a point and leads to somewhere important. It is important to listen when the Inspector is speaking as often the things he says foreshadow other issues. For example, "Do you want me to tell you, in plain words?" Inspector Goole is patronising towards the family, he treats them as if they are idiots and he sometimes treats them as if they are young children, still sheltered from the world they are living in. The language he uses is often commanding, short and very intelligent.

From the beginning of the play Priestley makes the audience dislike Birling as a character. This is what the playwright wanted to achieve as he wanted the capitalist to be the 'bad guy' and the socialist a good guy, so that he could get his message across effectively. This makes the play didactic. Birling is self-obsessed and oblivious to the world around him, so Priestley makes him the villain in the play. For example, "She had a lot to say-far to much-so she had to go." Arthur Birling is unaware of the poor people surrounding him, or maybe he just turns a blind eye towards it. He doesn't seem to care that people are suffering and dying, as long as he's safe and his money's safe then he is happy. He is a character the audience instantly dislike and he is a character who none of the audience can sympathise with throughout the play.

In complete contrast to Mr. Birling, Inspector Goole has a lot of moral values. His character is mysterious throughout the play and the name "Goole" could be a reference to the word "ghoul", meaning ghost or spirit. He sees the world as it really is and plans to do something about the people in the world who are suffering. He strongly dislikes Mr. Birling and his family, as they are too stuck in their class to even think about all the poor people in the world. The Inspector is a very powerful figure in the play and also he is a vital role, as without the Inspector there would be no one to compare Mr. Birling to. For example, "Public men, Mr Birling, have responsibilities as well as privileges". The

Inspector sees it as his duty to educate these people and try and change their view of the world as well as their attitudes towards other people. When I went to see the play of "An Insepctor Calls" Shelia came right out of the house and onto the street, when the Inspector questioned her. This was to signify that he had taught her a lesson and she was now willing to step out of her comfort zone and help people less well off than her.

Overall, I feel the contrast between the Inspector and Mr. Birling is a very important part of the play as they are both the two extremes. Mr. Birling is too wrapped up in his own life to care about anyone else and the Inspector cares about other people and is passionate about his job. In the play, J.B. Priestley gets across his message, cleverly encoded inside the acting. As a result, the audience dislike Mr. Birling and see the Inspector as some kind of role model, or hero. I think that had it been a capitalist writing the play, they could just as easily have made Mr. Birling the "good guy" and the Inspector dislikeable. So I think that although Mr. Birling and the Inspector are very different characters from each other and conflict within the play, they are so different that they are actually quite similar, and a clever writer could easily turn the play around to make Mr. Birling a character who people respect a lot.

Teaching & revision ideas

Arranging and re-arranging the characters into different groupings
highlights features they have in common and features that
distinguish them from each other. Write the name of each
character, including off-stage and minor ones, such as Alderman
Meggarty and Colonel Roberts, on a piece of paper and cut them out
individually. Now turn over the paper and mix the pieces into a pile.
Turn over three pieces at random. Put two characters together and
separate one from this pair. Write down or discuss your justification.
Now try to group them in a different way. For example, if you turned
up Sheila, Gerald and Meggarty, the first two could be grouped as a
couple and as on-stage major characters, excluding Meggarty. But
Meggarty and Gerald are both male and both were at bar of the
Brumley Palace music hall and met Eva/ Daisy there. Once you've
exhausted different ways of arranging these three, place the pieces of
paper back in the pile, shuffle and pick another three. Repeat the
process for as long as it is productive. Work either on your own or in a
pair.

Re-creative writing involves stepping into the shoes of the writer and
making the kinds of decisions writers make, practising the kinds
of craft writers practise. It's a great, usually enjoyable way of
getting to know and appreciate any writer's style. Add a scene to *An
Inspector Calls*.

What, for instance could happen after the final phone call? Or write scenes that are only reported in the play, such as those between Eva and Gerald and the Birlings. When some actors are on stage, others are not. In the fictional world of the play, these characters are imagined as doing something else while the main action continues on stage. Imagine the conversation between Mrs. Birling and Sheila when they first leave the dining-room, or between Mr. Birling and Eric in Eric's bedroom.

Often in a play what characters are not saying is as important as what they are saying. Take a scene of a few pages and complete a thought-tracking exercise. Stop the action every few lines and try to imagine what might be going through the minds of all the characters present, especially perhaps those who are not currently speaking much. If you're working with another pupil in a class, you could read out the character's thoughts and peers could try to guess which character you are tracking and when they might be having these thoughts.

Whose thoughts, for example, do you think the following might be and when? 'Just smile and bear it. But, oh, he's such a patronising so-and-so, that one, isn't he? A bit of a bully too, to be honest, puffed up and full of himself, especially tonight. And the pay's not great – the going rate, as he so likes to say. What's the going rate for the money he makes, that's what I'd like to know. But it is work and that's something to be grateful for, especially in times like these. That's it, you help yourself to a little more grog, as usual. Don't mind me. Impress the young man, why don't you?

Those two make a nice pair, mind. Spoilt, mind you, born with a silver spoon and all that, but a handsome pair, nevertheless, you can't deny. And she means well, really, even if she is spoilt, especially compared to her, Mrs. B. It's not nice to say, but she's a dragon really. Of course, no problem, at your service, yes sir, no sir, if I had a cap I'd doff it. Delighted to be of help.'

A character's speech: Imagine that after the end of the play the main characters are going to be interviewed by a new police inspector. Without using the text, write a short speech by each character in their voice outlining their interactions with Eva. You'll need to decide beforehand what they will and will not reveal.

Take a short section of the play, a few pages long, and prepare a performance of it to be broadcast as a radio programme. After your first read through, think through all the different dimensions of sound you can utilise, such as single and multiple voices, volume, pitch, tone and pacing. Try to identify the most climactic moment in your extract and build towards this, for example, by reading more quickly and loudly as you move towards it. If you're brave enough, record your section and listen to it critically.

Take the same or another short section from the play and imagine you were going to direct a stage production. Write detailed notes on the scene on how you would like the actors to play their roles. Include proxemics, costumes, accents, tone. Make sure you provide advice on what the actors should be doing when they are on stage but their character is not speaking – where they should sit or what their posture should be, what body language they display, who or what are they looking at and so forth.

Also write notes on your stage design, lighting and sound effects.

The unbelievable truth. Write a short speech of around one side A4 in the voice of one of the play's principle characters. Though you should try to imitate the way the character's speech is rendered by Priestley most of what they say should be wildly inaccurate and factually incorrect. Except that is for five true things you'll try to bury within your speech. The aim is to read your speech to someone else without them being able to spot the five truths among all the nonsense.

Imagine you have been commissioned to produce a radically new production of the play. Brainstorm staging and costume ideas. For instance, consider how you could use lighting and/ or music to make the Inspector appear more mysterious and ghostly. How could you emphasise the ideas of guilt, confession and potential absolution? How might you emphasise the play's political message? How or why might you include an actor playing Eva Smith into a production? The crazier and more imaginative the ideas, the better. How about an out-of-scale large door to the living-room and an oversized telephone? How about swapping the characters' genders? Once you've finished, consider whether Priestley's play can, in fact, be radically re-imagined, or whether it has to be played a certain way.

GLOSSARY

ALENATION EFFECT – coined by German playwright, Berthold Brecht, it reverses the conventional idea that audience's suspend their disbelief when watching a play

ANTITHESIS – the use of balanced opposites, at sentence or text level

APOSTROPHE – a figure of speech addressing a person, object or idea

ASIDE – brief words spoken for only the audience to hear

CADENCE – the rise of fall of sounds in a line

CATHARSIS – a feeling of release an audience supposedly feels the end of a tragedy

CONCEIT – an extended metaphor

DRAMATIC IRONY – when the audience knows things the on-stage characters do not

FIGURATIVE LANGUAGE – language that is not literal, but employs figures of speech, such as metaphor, simile and personification

FOURTH WALL – the term for the invisible wall between the audience and the actors on the stage

GOTHIC – a style of literature characterised by psychological horror, dark deeds and uncanny events

HAMARTIA – a tragic or fatal flaw in the protagonist of a tragedy that contributes significantly to their downfall

HEROIC COUPLETS – pairs of rhymed lines in iambic pentameter

HYPERBOLE – extreme exaggeration

IAMBIC – a metrical pattern of a weak followed by a strong stress, ti-TUM, like a heart beat

IMAGERY – the umbrella term for description in poetry. Sensory imagery refers to descriptions that appeal to sight, sound and so forth; figurative imagery refers to the use of devices such as metaphor, simile and personification

JUXTAPOSITION – two things placed together to create a strong contrast

METAPHOR – an implicit comparison in which one thing is said to be another

METRE – the regular pattern organising sound and rhythm in a poem

MONOLOGUE – extended speech by a single character

MOTIF – a repeated image or pattern of language, often carrying thematic significance

ONOMATOPOEIA – bang, crash, wallop

PENTAMETER – a poetic line consisting of five beats

PERSONIFICATION – giving human characteristics to inanimate things

PLOSIVE – a type of alliteration using 'p' and 'b' sounds

ROMANTIC – a type of poetry characterised by a love of nature, by strong emotion and heightened tone

SIMILE – an explicit comparison of two different things

SOLILOQUY – a speech by a single character alone on stage revealing their innermost thoughts

STAGECRAFT – a term for all the stage devices used by a playwright, encompassing lighting, costume, music, directions and so forth

STICHOMYTHIA – quick, choppy exchanges of dialogue between characters

SUSPENSIOIN OF DISBELIEF – the idea that the audience willing treats the events on stage as if they were real

SYMBOL – something that stands in for something else. Often a concrete representation of an idea.

SYNTAX – the word order in a sentence. doesn't Without sense English syntax make. Syntax is crucial to sense: For example, though it uses all the same words, 'the man eats the fish' is not the same as 'the fish eats the man'

TRAGEDY – a play that ends with the deaths of the main characters

UNITIES – A description of tragic structure by Aristotle that relates to three elements of time, place and action

WELL-MADE PLAY – a type of play that follows specific conventions so that its action looks and feels realistic.

About the authors

Head of English and freelance writer, Neil Bowen has a Masters Degree in Literature & Education from Cambridge University and is a member of Ofqual's experts panel for English. He is the author of *The Art of Writing English Essays for GCSE*, co-author of *The Art of Writing English Essays for A-level and Beyond* and of *The Art of Poetry* series. Neil runs the peripeteia project, bridging the gap between A-level and degree level English courses www.peripeteia.webs.com, and delivers talks at GCSE & A-level student conferences for The Training Partnership.

After leading English departments in deprived parts of the country to outstanding progress, currently Jennie Brimming is an Assistant Principal, responsible for teaching and learning. Jennie holds a first class degree from Kingston University.

James Engineer is a Teach First participant and KS4 Coordinator for English at Torquay Academy. In 2017, James graduated from Oxford University with a first class degree in English Language and Literature.

Kathrine Mortimore is a Lead Practitioner at Torquay Academy. She has a Masters degree in Advanced Subject Teaching from Cambridge University where she focused on tackling disadvantage in the English classroom, a topic she has continued to blog about at: kathrinemortimore.wordpress.com.

Printed in Great Britain
by Amazon